Thinking like an Economist: A Guide to Rational Decision Making

Randall Bartlett, Ph.D.

THE
GREAT
COURSES®

PUBLISHED BY:

THE GREAT COURSES
Corporate Headquarters
4840 Westfields Boulevard, Suite 500
Chantilly, Virginia 20151-2299
Phone: 1-800-832-2412
Fax: 703-378-3819
www.thegreatcourses.com

Randall Bartlett, Ph.D.
Professor of Economics
Smith College

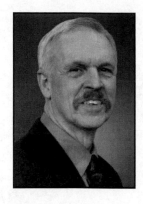

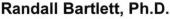

R andall Bartlett is Professor of Economics at Smith College, where he has taught for the past 30 years. A graduate of Occidental College, he earned his master's degree and doctorate from Stanford University. At Smith, Professor Bartlett has won 2 all-college teaching awards and the 2003 Distinguished Professor Award.

In addition to his regular duties in the Department of Economics, Professor Bartlett has been instrumental in developing a number of important programs at Smith. He was the first director of the program in public policy and devised, and for the first 10 years directed, the Phoebe Reese Lewis Leadership Program. He has for the past 5 years been the faculty coordinator of the Mellon Mays Undergraduate Fellowship program, an initiative to identify and encourage promising young scholars from underrepresented groups to attend graduate school. He has served at both the department and college levels as a teaching mentor for junior faculty.

Each fall he presents Financing Life, a wildly popular financial literacy lecture series attended by students, faculty, staff, and community members. He also conducts a 3-hour crash course on basic financial literacy for the senior class in the week just prior to graduation. He is currently the director of the Urban Studies program.

Prior to joining the faculty at Smith, Professor Bartlett taught at Williams College and the University of Washington. He also worked for the Federal Trade Commission for 2 years. He is the author of 3 books and numerous articles. His most recent book, *The Crisis of America's Cities*, explores the problems and prospects of urban America. ■

Table of Contents

Table of Contents

Thinking like an Economist:
A Guide to Rational Decision Making

Scope:

To think like an economist is to see the world in a unique way. Is it rational to commit a crime? Is it optimal to maintain an insurance policy on a car that's worth almost nothing? In this course, we will develop a tool kit to help you view the world through the economist's lens, enabling you to better understand the world around you and to improve your day-to-day decision making.

We begin to build our tool kit with 6 foundation principles that are manifested in virtually all human endeavors, from personal choices to global policies. These include examining any decision, yours or someone else's, in terms of incentives, seeing the world as a system with limited resources, and seeing all human interactions as interconnected and beyond careful control. Next we add the 3 core concepts that are always part of economic thinking: rationality, marginal analysis, and optimization.

We'll learn to apply our tool kit to situations as diverse as combating global warming and purchasing a snow blower. We'll see how rational individual choices can result in efficient social outcomes. But we'll also take a page from game theory and its prisoner's dilemma, in which interdependent rational decisions make both parties worse off. Environmental damage is an example of the tragedy of the commons, in which no one has a direct incentive to protect a public good but everyone suffers as a consequence. What do economists see as the solution to these problems?

We go on to examine the importance of information and risk in rational decision making. No amount of information is sufficient for us to be certain about some outcomes, so we use the concept of expected value to make optimal decisions. What if the information you need is known and controlled by someone else—someone who has a stake in your decision? We learn how to navigate the world of information asymmetry, found, among other places, in retail shopping, job searches, and political campaigns. We then factor in the impact of timing, the value of money, and psychology. The field of behavioral economics introduces us to many well-documented, but puzzling, behaviors that seem inconsistent with what we've learned about rational decision making. We will learn how human psychology sometimes leads to our making unexpected or less than optimal decisions. We wrap up our course by exploring ways to devise incentives for ourselves to overcome some of our behavioral irrationality.

By the end of the course, you should have a clear understanding of what it means to think like an economist. You will have internalized a mental tool kit you can apply to personal, work, and political decisions. This approach will help you better understand the motivations of others and of yourself—and to optimize the decisions you make. ■

The Economist's Tool Kit—6 Principles
Lecture 1

The *New York Times* nonfiction bestseller lists have really been extraordinary for economists in recent years. ... There have been a number of books about how economists think. ... These aren't books about success in business; they're not books about investing for wealth. ... Steven Levitt and Stephen Dubner's *Freakonomics*, Tim Harford's *The Logic of Life*, and Richard Thaler and Cass Sunstein's book *Nudge*, among others. ... At first glance it seems strange that so many seemingly rational people have made that choice. Or is it? Perhaps it's that the authors have finally been able to communicate the power of thinking like an economist.

There's a certain essence of what it means to think like an economist. When made comprehensible, economic thinking can be incredibly powerful and useful in understanding the world, in making personal decisions, in formulating business strategies, or in choosing national policy. Developing your ability to make these evaluations more effectively is the objective of this course. Once you learn to think like an economist, you will never be quite the same again.

To think like an economist is to view the world from the 6 foundation principles of economic thinking. Principle number 1: People respond to incentives. No premise is more central: If you reward a behavior, people will do more of it and more intensely; if you penalize it, they'll do less of it. If you tax cigarettes more, people will smoke less. If you offer free breakfast, people will line up around the block.

People respond to incentives: Taxing cigarettes decreases sales.

Principle number 2: There is no such thing as a free lunch. It sounds silly, but that expression captures a lot of economic thought. When economists look at the world, they see an unavoidable imbalance between the wants we have on one hand and the limited resources we have on the other. A fundamental reality is that there is always going to be scarcity: Any use of time or limited resources for one purpose is an opportunity forever gone to use them for another. More of anything always means less of something else; and it's that option that you had to give up that economists call **opportunity cost**.

Principle number 3: No thing is just one thing; there are always at least 2 sides to every interaction. I recently read a column arguing that it was unethical for those of us who had jobs in a period of economic difficulty to continue spending when others are unemployed. But the reality is that every dollar of my expenditure is a dollar of income coming in for someone else. If there's less total spending, there's also by definition less total income.

Principle number 4: The law of unanticipated influences. We can see this with a concept from chaos theory called the **butterfly effect**. In chaos theory, hypothetically, a butterfly on one side of the world can flap its wings and, through a chain of causation that's totally unpredictable, cause a hurricane on the opposite side of the world. This is true in economics: No event ever takes place in a bubble; a change in any one part of an economic system is going to have ripple effects, often in far removed places. The 1979 embassy takeover in Tehran, Iran, resulted in an increase in dental costs in the United States. How does that happen? There was fear that there might be war in the Middle East, which could result in the disruption of financial markets. People turned to gold and silver as a hedge against this uncertainty, which impacted the costs of dental fillings and X-ray film. Butterfly effects are real: We are often impacted by things we cannot anticipate or control.

Principle number 5: The law of unintended consequences. In our interconnected world, our actions are always going to have multiple consequences. A number of cities have installed red light cameras, which take a photograph of the license plate of any car that enters an intersection after the light has turned red. The intended purpose, of course, was to reduce the number of intersection accidents. The cameras achieved this, but they also increased the number of rear-end accidents caused by people slamming on their brakes to avoid the cameras.

Principle number 6: No one is, and no one ever can be, in complete control. If you apply an incentive to some subset of 6 billion complexly interrelated people, whose interactions are totally unforeseeable and have unintended consequences, and then predict the final result, that would be monumental. To go further and try to control that outcome would be utterly impossible.

When economists approach any problem, they are grounded in a paradigm defined by these 6 principles. At face value, they are simple, but they can be applied in endless contexts. Their richness comes not from the complexity of the vision but from their adaptability to so many different situations. ■

Important Terms

butterfly effect: In chaos theory, the hypothesis that small events can be linked through distant causal chains to seemingly unrelated events (e.g., the beating of a butterfly's wings would theoretically set in motion a chain of events that would lead to a change in a distant weather pattern).

opportunity cost: The value of the next-best thing that must be given up when time or resources are devoted to one use. It is what is forgone.

Take-Away Points

1. Economists look to the incentives facing decision makers to predict, explain, or prescribe their choices and behavior. Incentives are key.

2. In a world of scarcity, nothing is truly free. There is always a cost in terms of opportunities forgone, even if not in terms of money.

The Economist's Tool Kit—6 Principles
Lecture 1—Transcript

Hello. I want to welcome you to this course on *How to Think Like an Economist*. My name's Randy Bartlett; I'm currently a professor of Economics at Smith College in Northampton, Massachusetts. For longer than I really care to admit I've been teaching economics at colleges and universities throughout the nation, and during that time it's occurred to me that there's a certain essence, a core, of what it means to think like an economist. Over the course of the next 12 lectures I'm going to try to share that thinking with you. We're going to pay some special attention to the concept of rationality in decision making, and whether you're making personal, business, or policy choices.

The *New York Times* nonfiction bestseller lists have really been extraordinary for economists in recent years. There have been the normal stories of surviving mountaineering disasters; there have been the tales of horrid crimes and the hardworking journalists, detectives, and lawyers who have all solved them; there have been books about the newest diets and the celebrities who adhere to them; but what has been most unusual about this is there have been a number of books about how economists think. "Economic thinking" volumes on the bestseller lists, some for months at a time? Not since 1848, when Thomas Carlyle first dubbed economics the "The Dismal Science" have economics books enjoyed that kind of popularity. These aren't books about "success in business"; they're not books about "investing for wealth"; generally economics books are like discrete mathematics textbooks: They're interesting to a few, but not likely to achieve top-seller status. Yet there they are: Steven Levitt and Stephen Dubner's *Freakonomics*, Tim Harford's *The Logic of Life*, Richard Thaler and Cass Sunstein's book *Nudge*, among others.

Except in the economics textbook market, "best-selling economics book" has been kind of an oxymoron. Students, of course, buy them because they have to; adults buy them only when they choose to; and at first glance it seems strange that so many seemingly rational people have made that choice. Or is it? Perhaps it's that the authors have finally been able to communicate the power of thinking like an economist. When I've covered a particularly difficult task in economics sometimes, I joke with my students and say, "You know, economics is really the art of making common sense incomprehensible." But these books seem to be evidence that when it's made comprehensible, people get to see how incredibly powerful and useful it can be in understanding the world, in making personal decisions, in formulating business strategies, or choosing national policy. Developing your ability to do all that more effectively is the ultimate objective of this course.

Last summer, I had one of those rare moments in the Pacific Northwest. It was a beautiful, clear night and the sun was setting behind the Olympic Mountains; it was one of those truly magical moments. But for just a second I was struck by the realization that if I had a geologist on one side of me and an artist on the other looking at the exact same scene they would literally "see" different things than I saw, or that each other saw. We all see the world through particular "lenses"; we all have a particular perspective, a way that helps us understand the "raw data" that we confront. I think professional training in any field forever changes what you see in the world; indeed, that's what it means to become a professional. If confronted with facts about global warming, a lawyer's going to say, "This is legal issues," but non-lawyers will not see them. Biologists will immediately be drawn to impacts, invisible to the rest of us, on life forms. Political scientists will immediately see that this is a question of interest group politics and treaty enforcement.

There's a term in common usage now that has to do with re-visioning the world, seeing it as a different place, and that term is "paradigm shift." Thomas Kuhn was perhaps the first to use that term, "paradigm shift," in his book *The Structure of Scientific Revolutions*. For Kuhn, a "paradigm" is a shared explanation and understanding of the world. To be inducted into a community of scientists is to accept its paradigm; and once there, practitioners truly live in a different world. Economists are no different: To become an economist is to see the world through a particular lens. It shapes what you see; it focuses your attention; it illuminates particular solutions to complex problems. Once you learn to think like an economist, you will never be quite the same again. Mostly, I think that's a good thing. In this series of lectures, I hope to give you an entrée into the economists' paradigm, so that you can see and understand the world as economists do, and perhaps even behave differently within it.

Let's begin with what I'm going to call the "Six Foundation Principles of Economic Thinking." These precepts are so fully melded into an economists' mind that they're not even aware of thinking about them at many times. There's no reason to defend or articulate them, they're just part of reality; they define the world in which economists "live." Then in the next lecture, we'll talk about three "Core Concepts": "marginal analysis," "rationality," and "optimization," which is sometimes also called "constrained maximization." When we have all that combined, we're really going to have pretty much the complete basic toolkit of thinking like an economist. Then with these six principles, plus the three concepts, economists believe they're incredibly well-equipped to predict and to explain human behavior. And more: They also think they have ways to prescribe ways to make our decisions more "efficient." Then, that's about it; we'll have all the basic tools, and what we'll do is we'll apply those tools in different contexts in ever more complex variations.

Let's turn now to these Foundation Principles. Anyone who's taken physics knows that Sir Isaac Newton was able to take the three fundamental laws of motion, express them simply and elegantly, and contain a tremendous amount of truth. Ours principles are going to be less mathematically precise than Newton's, perhaps less quantifiable; but they, too, are very much at the heart of what it means: Dress them up, apply them in fancy contexts, give them different names; but to think like an economist is to view the world from the foundation of these principles.

Principle Number One: People respond to incentives. No premise is more central: If you reward a behavior, people will do more of it and more intensely; penalize an act, and they'll do less of it. If you tax cigarettes more, people will smoke less. If you offer free breakfast, as Denny's did the morning after Super Bowl XLIII, people will line up around the block. If you urge people to retire their gas guzzlers, some will do so; but if you create a "Cash for Clunkers" program, as the government did, 700,000 cars get turned in, in one month. If you make people wait in a gas line for two hours to get gas, as so many of us had to do in the 1970s, public transit ridership will go up. If you make the proportion of classes that have more than 50 students in them a negative factor in the formula for *U.S. News and World Report's* ranking of colleges, some colleges will suddenly start capping all their classes at 49.

Policy makers think like economists sometime when they're making policy, and when they do they should take time to consider the incentives. If you subsidize home ownership, as the IRS code does through the mortgage interest deduction and the property tax deduction, you will get more home ownership. If you tax anything—whether we're talking about payrolls, healthcare premiums, or capital gains—you're going to get less of it.

If you ask an economist, "Tell me about criminal activity," she will not tell you anything about breakdowns in social mores; she instead is going to focus her attention on the payoffs that come from "honest" effort compared to the payoffs that come from crime. She'll talk about the penalties, the costs, of crime; she'll talk about the probabilities of arrest and conviction; but because she is thinking like an economist when she looks at criminal behavior, she's going to see crime as a response to incentives the potential criminals face. If you ask an economist about the development of new vaccines, there will be almost no conversation about the molecular structure of viruses. No, there will be, instead, a substantial discussion of the costs of doing research, the probabilities of successful discovery, the terms of patent protection, the questions of potential liability. What's going to be the Rate of Innovation? That's going to depend upon the incentives that pharmaceutical companies, their competitors, and their potential customers face. Principle One is: Human behavior is not random; intentionally or unintentionally, it's strategic. People respond to incentives; if you change the incentives, behavior will respond. Thinking like an economist doesn't mean just thinking about our own "optimal" response to our own incentives; it also means we need to think ahead and anticipate how our decisions and our actions affect the incentives that other people will face, and what kind of reactions we'll get as a result.

These stories may be apocryphal, but they're certainly fun to listen to. They're stories that were told about the kind of wasteful production that took place in the old Soviet Union when it was still a planned economy. The central planning authority would issue directives to the managers of the plants, telling them what to produce. There are stories of how ill-designed incentives led to ridiculous outcomes. If they told the manager he'd be rewarded for the tons of nails that he produced, then you could imagine what would happen: you got the biggest, heaviest nails possible being produced.

If you told the manager, "We're going to give you rewards based on the number of nails you produced," you can, again, imagine the consequence: they'll produce the tiniest little nails they can in order to produce as many as possible. People respond to incentives; Principle Number One.

Principle Number Two: There is no such thing as a free lunch. Sounds silly, but that captures a lot of economic thought. If you go to any introductory textbook, it probably has a subtitle: "Economics, the science of choice." When economists look at the world, they see an unavoidable imbalance between the wants we have on one hand and the limited resources we have on the other. One of the first lessons that any infant must learn is that Mick Jagger was right when he sang, "You can't always get what you want. That's true for individuals; that's true for organizations; that's true for natures. I don't know whether that wisdom came to Mick Jagger because of his life experience, or perhaps even from his years studying at the London School of Economics; but whatever the source, a fundamental reality in the economists' world is that there is always going to be some kind of scarcity. The consequence of scarcity is that means there is always going to be a cost.

My wife and I, like many Americans, subscribe to Netflix, and that means that our queue moves along and there are always two or three DVDs waiting on the counter for an evening when there's nothing better to do. Not long ago, we took one that had arrived—we both claimed the other one must have ordered it—and we watched it all the way through; and I'll be honest with you, it was awful. We should have turned it off; but no, we watched it all the way through. At the end, my wife—who is a terrific and brilliant physician, but not well-trained in economics—said, "Well, at least we didn't have to pay for it." "Au contraire," I said—exhausting all of my working knowledge of French—"you and I both spent two hours of our limited lives watching that, and we can never get them back, and we paid: Other options, things we could have done with that time, are now forever gone to us."

A generalizable characteristic of the "no free lunch" world is this fact of "scarcity." "Scarcity" means that any use of time or limited resources for one purpose is an opportunity forever gone to use them for another. More of anything always means less of something else; and it's that lost option, it's what you had to give up, that is the real or what economists call "opportunity cost." Cost is never "money"; money's an abstract unit we can use to quantify things. But the real cost is always the lost opportunity. If you buy the car, you have to forego the boat. If you spend your vacation skiing, the "cost" is that you can't spend your vacation at the beach. If you spend four years in medical school, it means you're not going to be in art school (or, I suppose, driving a garbage truck). The older I get, the more I appreciate the harsh reality in the query "How are you spending your time?" Even when no money changes hands, we're always incurring some very real costs.

Economists always recognize this. Others of think of cost in terms of money spent, cash laid out. I remember back in the 1980s when short-term interest rates were over 20 percent, and I was having a conversation with the manager of one of the local lumber yards. I said to him, "Interest rates that high, they must be hammering you." "Not at all," he said, "We self-finance; we don't have to borrow for inventory, these interest rates are really costing us nothing." You and I can see the flaw in his thinking: Interest rates at that level meant that every $100 he has tied up in inventory meant he had to be giving up the opportunity to earn more than $20 a year by lending that money out. Passing up receiving a gain, in the world of rational decision making, is the same as paying it out; both are costs. An accountant's going to think of money out; an economist will always see a cost in giving up an opportunity: money that does not come in, value that is not gained. More and more Americans these days are being asked to decide what to do with their 401k investment accounts. An astonishing number of young workers, decades away from retirement, are deciding to put all of their funds into a "safe" money market account; after all, you can't lose. But of course you can: There's an opportunity cost. By investing conservatively in their youth, they're probably giving up tens of thousands of dollars in lost appreciation. The "security" they're getting, like the apparently "free" lunch, isn't really free at all.

Principle Number Three: No thing is just one thing; there are always (at least) two sides to every interaction. Economics, after all, is one of the social sciences. It likes to call itself the "queen of the social sciences"—most people don't, but economists like to do that—and when people interact, there's always more than one side to the interaction. For example, not long ago in our local newspaper there was a letter to the editor talking about climate change, and the author said, "We are never going to solve the problem of global warming until we have all sold our big, fuel-gulping SUVs and bought fuel efficient automobiles." Good sentiment, bad reasoning, because we cannot sell our SUVs unless someone else buys our SUVs, and in that case all that happens is the big cars change driveways; the world, as a whole, is unaffected.

I also recently read a column that was arguing that it was unethical for those of us who had jobs in a period of economic difficultly to continue spending when others are unemployed. "In solidarity, we should forego our purchases," the column said, "until the economic crisis is solved." But the result of that, of course—if you think it about it—is that would let more people have experience with unemployment firsthand, because every single dollar of my expenditure on the other side is a dollar of income coming in. If there's less total spending, there's also by definition less total income. No thing is just one thing. Every sale is also a purchase; every dollar of spending is also a dollar of income; every import is an export. A change in the incentives for one person is a change in the incentives for someone else.

The fourth principle I like to call the Law of Unanticipated Influences, but it arises from something out of chaos theory called the "Butterfly Effect." In chaos theory, hypothetically, a butterfly on one side of the world can flap its wings and through a chain of causation that's totally unanticipatable it'll result in a hurricane on the opposite side of the world. I know in economics it's true, because no event ever takes place in a bubble; a change in any one part of an economic system is going to have ripple effects, often in far removed places. In 1979, the student radicals took over the embassy in Tehran, Iran, and the result was that dental costs in the United States were pushed higher. I think you're probably asking yourself, "How does that happen?" It goes like this: There was a lot of political uncertainty in the world, and there was fear that there might be war in the Middle East. The consequence of that would be that financial markets would be disrupted, and there was an uncertainty in financial markets and a flight to gold and silver as a hedge against this uncertainty. Gold and silver are financial assets; but they're also used in crowns in teeth, silver is used in fillings, and silver is the most expensive component of x-ray film. I'll tell you: It's a rare manager in a Human Resources department who, reading the news that day, knew that

that distant crisis on the far side of the world would be the thing that would explode his benefits budget in the coming year; but it did.

In the American Civil War, the Union forces adopted a strategy they called the "anaconda strategy." They put a blockade around the Southern ports, and the consequence of that was that rents far away in Birmingham, England were driven down, and land prices in Egypt were driven up. Cut off from supplies of raw cotton, the Birmingham mills cut back on their employment; the wages for the workers fell; with their lower incomes, they had less demand for housing and could afford lower rent. Meanwhile, the suppliers were looking for substitute sources of raw cotton, and Egypt has a favorable climate for cotton growing. The demand for land in Egypt went up; the price for land in Egypt went up; and forever that North African economy has been reshaped.

In the California housing market collapse in 2008, the foreclosures in the Central Valley of California caused English cities to cut back on their police patrols. How does that happen? The British towns had been keeping their funds in Icelandic banks because they were paying higher interest rates. The banks, in turn, were using those funds to invest in derivatives—something called Collateralized Debt Obligations—that were based on subprime U.S. mortgages. When the housing prices in California fell, the Collateralized Debt Obligations became unsalable, the Icelandic banks failed, and the British cities lost the money in their accounts and had to reduce public services, including police patrols in Birmingham.

Butterfly effects are real. We will often be impacted by things we cannot anticipate and cannot control. Be ever vigilant; trust no one when they tell you that they have accounted for all eventualities, for no one ever has.

The fifth principle is one that I'm going to call The Law of Unintended Consequences: Not only is it impossible for us to anticipate all the things that will affect us from the outside, in our interconnected world, our actions are also always going to have multiple consequences. Economic thinking can help you perhaps anticipate them. A number of cities have installed what they call "red light cameras," where they take a photograph of the license plate of any car that enters an intersection after the light has turned red.

Citations are mailed to the owners; and the intended purpose, of course, was to try and reduce the number of intersection accidents. They did; but they also increased the number of rear end accidents, an unintended consequence of people slamming on their brakes to try and avoid the red light cameras.

In 2008, Nebraska passed a "safe-haven" statute. Its purpose was to prevent the all-too-common tragedy of a desperate teen becoming pregnant, delivering a baby, panicking, and doing harm to her newborn infant. Nebraska's safe haven law said that any child dropped off at a hospital, police station, or fire station would be accepted, no questions asked. But the language said "child," not infant; and the result was that a number of the parents of troubled teens, when they'd run out of patience, dropped their kids off at a hospital and drove away. There were even cases of people coming from out of state to drive away from their "problem" as the teenager stood on the hospital steps. There was carelessness when they were failing to consider how what they were doing might affect the decisions of others, and lead to an outcome that was both unintended and in many senses tragic.

Certainly businesses are not exempt from this. As an exercise, let's try thinking like economists about a recent case study. Some of the airlines, citing difficult market conditions, decided that they were going to charge checked baggage fees. If you think like an economist, the first result is obvious: that means some people will simply choose another airline. That's pretty easy; the next step is easy, too, but I'm not sure it was taken by the airlines themselves. What about the people who continue to fly on the airline? They've now been given an incentive to carry on as much luggage as possible. In effect, the airline says, "We'll pay you $25 to carry your luggage down that jetway." But there's no increase in bin capacity, and that leads to interesting possibilities.

I had a friend who took a trip right after these charges were introduced, and she reported that this was the following: They boarded by group, as we often do in jetways, and at the end of Group Two's boarding the ground crew came out and said, "I'm sorry, all of the overhead bins are completely full, and everyone else will have to gate check their luggage on the jetway one at a time before boarding." The passengers were upset as you can imagine, so to assuage them the ground crew said, "But we won't charge you the baggage fee." One by one the bags were tagged and hand carried down stairs; there was a 45 minute delay. They did not collect any fees on most of the luggage that did get checked; the passengers who paid the checking fee were angry because they had to pay; the gate checked people were angry because they didn't have the convenience of carry on; everyone experienced a 45 minute delay. There was an angry load of passengers as they went across the way. It must have seemed like a good idea at the time, but it's only because no one at the airline apparently thought through to work all the incentive changes and how they could have such obvious, but I'm sure unintended, consequences.

The last principle: Finally, given all of the above, assuming it's true, no one is, and no one ever can be, in complete control. "It's not rocket science"; that's what we say when we want to put a problem in context; we want to say, "It's not that difficult." But what we've said above says that thinking like an economist may sometimes actually be harder than doing rocket science, because in physics, if you apply a given force in a given direction to a given mass, the outcome is pretty much always the same. But if you apply an incentive to some subset of six billion complexly interrelated people, whose interactions are totally unforeseeable, whose actions have unintended consequences, and then try to predict the final result, that would be monumental. To go further and try to control that outcome would be utterly impossible. In the final analysis, no one is in control.

In conclusion, if we sum this all up: When an economist approaches any problem, he or she is grounded in a paradigm, a world vision, defined by these six principles. At face value, they're pretty simple: People respond to incentives. To think like an economist, you always have to consider how. In a world of scarcity, there is no free lunch; there will always be an opportunity cost to be paid. There are no real free lunches. You can never do just one thing; each interaction has at least two sides; nothing is every just one thing. Everything is so interconnected that there will always be unanticipated influences and impacts; things will come to affect us that we cannot even begin to imagine. The fifth one is that our actions will sometimes have unintended consequences, and of that we need to be aware. When all of that is said and done, when all of that is struck, no one is truly in control.

These principles define what it means to "think like an economist." There really isn't much more to it than that; and perhaps you'd liked to have known that before you signed on for the whole course. Nevertheless, these principles are about it, but they can be applied in oh-so-many different contexts; and the richness comes not from the complexity of the vision but from its adaptability to so many different situations. Next time, we'll add to these principles three Core Concepts, and then our basic toolkit will be nearly complete; and the fun is going to be in learning to use these tools in so many different ways.

The Economist's Tool Kit—3 Core Concepts
Lecture 2

No one who's read both Charles Dickens and Ernest Hemingway will ever confuse one with the other. As artists, their styles were reflections of themselves and reflections of the times in which they wrote; and perhaps also, in some small measure at least, they were reflections in the way they were paid. Most of Dickens's novels were serialized, usually in about 20 parts, and he would receive a contract payment every time he filled up 32 pages of printed text. ... Hemingway, of course, got paid by the completed manuscript. There was no financial incentive for him to modify his sparse style of writing. ... Thinking like an economist means being ever cognizant of the incentives you face.

The 3 core analytic concepts in economics are **rationality**, marginal analysis, and **optimization**. Economists believe in rationality: They build extraordinarily complex models on the assumption that humans are fundamentally rational in their behavior. People will choose strategically rather than randomly. In principle, making rational decisions means following 4 simple steps: First, clarify the objective. Second, identify all possible alternative paths to achieve the objective. Third, evaluate carefully the payoffs from each of those alternatives. This is where economic thinking can help a lot—developing tools to help you understand how to put value on difficult things. Fourth, select the best option and implement your decision. In our world of scarcity, evaluating alternatives is all about valuing the opportunity costs. Rationality says that you should always choose the option with the highest

People make rational decisions by weighing alternatives.

Jochen Sand/Photodisc/Thinkstock.

net payoff; to knowingly choose anything worse would be irrational. The presumption of rationality works 2 ways: It helps us with the prediction and the description of behavior, and it also gives us a way to evaluate after the fact and draw conclusions about values. The concept of strategic decision making and rationality as both an objective for and a description of human behavior is fundamental to economic thinking.

The concept of strategic decision making and rationality as both an objective for and a description of human behavior is fundamental to economic thinking.

The second core concept is marginal analysis. Economists tend to look carefully at sequences of small changes made on the margin, because most of the choices we make in life are not all-or-nothing decisions; most of them involve marginal trade-offs. A little more of one thing inevitably means a little less of another. If we woke up tomorrow and gas prices had doubled, how would that affect automobile usage? As the **marginal value** changes, more of something makes the marginal value fall; less of something makes the marginal value rise. At high gas prices, some trips would not be worth it, but others certainly still would be. Thinking like an economist means we reject claims that a change in price is going to make things stop altogether. People adjust on the margin until the value of the last trip taken reflects the new, higher costs of driving.

The third core concept is about optimization in the equimarginal principle. This means figuring out the best attainable allocation given a set of constraints. Imagine yourself on a new TV reality show. You're flown by helicopter deep into the wilderness, with nothing but the clothes on your back. You're given 4 chits that you get to exchange for units of food or units of shelter. If you think like an economist, you're going to realize that survival is not about either food or shelter; it's about the best attainable combination of the two. Gorging on food while freezing to death is not a good strategy; basking in warmth and comfort while starving to death is not either. The optimal solution is to find the balance between food and shelter that will make the marginal value of each of them equal; hence the name "equimarginal principle."

Applying the concepts of rationality, marginal thinking, and optimization in a world proscribed by the 6 foundation principles means you are thinking like an economist. Complex econometric models are based on these essential ideas. Thinking like an economist means being aware of the incentives you face and, perhaps more importantly, the incentives those around you face. It means anticipating what's strategically rational for them, and how that will affect your options. It means focusing on the margin, on trade-offs, and on adjustments to find the optimal balance. The question is always how much? And of which? ■

Important Terms

marginal value: The change in a starting total value from a slight increase or decrease in an activity. If a bus company provides service between 2 cities, the marginal cost is the addition to cost of taking on 1 more passenger. The marginal revenue is the increase in revenue from selling the final ticket.

optimization (a.k.a. **constrained maximization**): The process of deriving as much benefit as possible within a given limit, for example, deriving the maximum possible benefit from a fixed income.

rationality: In economics, rationality means always choosing from among available options the one that provides the greatest net gain. It refers to the process of making choices, not to the objective sought.

Take-Away Points

1. Economic rationality refers to the process of reaching decisions: clarifying the goal, identifying and valuing all alternatives, and selecting the one with the highest net payoff.

2. Optimization comes from making small, sequential trade-offs and adjustments until there is a balance of marginal costs and benefits. Life's decisions are not either/or; they are about doing more or less of something.

The Economist's Tool Kit—3 Core Concepts
Lecture 2—Transcript

Welcome back for the second lecture in our series on "How to Think Like an Economist." If you'll recall in the last lecture, we talked about Six Foundation Principles; fundamental premises that all economists accept about humans and their social interactions. The first, of course, was that people respond to their incentives. The second was that in a world of scarcity, there is no free lunch; there's always going to be an opportunity cost to be paid. The third was that you can never do just one thing; every interaction has at least two sides. The fourth was that everything is interconnected; there can be unanticipated influences. The fifth was that actions are going to have unintended consequences. The last was that no one is ever truly in control. Together, these define the boundaries of the world in which economists live. Thinking, deciding, and acting like an economist means starting with that foundation.

Today, we're going to complete the Basic Economist Toolkit by developing three core analytic concepts: rationality, marginal analysis, and optimization, that we also sometimes call "constrained maximization." If you were to do a word search on a substantive economic article, I would expect the three most commonly recurring terms would be "rational," "marginal," and "optimal." Economists throw those words around like teenagers throw around the word "like." A working understanding of these three concepts and how economists use them is the goal for getting us through the lecture today; and then we're going to be equipped to talk about any issue and think like an economist about it.

First of all, economists believe in rationality; they build extraordinarily complex models on the assumption that humans are fundamentally "rational" in their behavior. That means that they're going to choose strategically rather than randomly; they sometimes stray, but strategic rationality is a strong working approximation of human behavior. But it's important to remember that economist's concept of rationality is much narrower than that of philosopher's. We make no judgments about the wisdom of your final objectives; we make no judgments about the goals; each person gets to decide what he or she really wants. What economists concern themselves with are the decision processes that people use when they're trying to obtain those objectives. Economic "rationality" refers to the process of decision making, not to its objective; people can rationally pursue ends that to others seem absolutely absurd.

Every winter where we live we drive past a frozen ox-bow lake along the Connecticut River. It's often covered with fishermen even on the coldest of days. They're sitting on stools, exposed, out on the ice; there they sit staring into a hole in the ice at a monofilament line for hours on end. My wife, who grew up in Arizona and has not been truly warm since we moved to New England, thinks they are crazy. "What rational person would ever choose to do that?" she asks. As an economist, I have to say any person who for whatever reason derives real pleasure from the experience should do that. If for whatever incomprehensible reason it brings them pleasure, it would be irrational for them not to be sitting there; for my wife, however, it would be absurd and irrational. Both the fishermen and my wife can make "rational" choices; what differs for them is the personal assessment of the experience.

It's how we decide, not what we decide, that marks rationality in the economist's view of the world. This can go to extraordinary extremes: If you were a true believer, as a suicide bomber, and you thought that God's will really required that you commit this unspeakable act, if you thought it would really bring immeasurable and eternal rewards in paradise, it could be "rational" in the economist's use of the term to push that detonator button. To me, as a human, that would be tragically mistaken, unquestionably immoral and unspeakably evil; but it would not, in formal terms, be irrational.

In principle, then, making rational decisions is easy; just follow four simple steps: First, clarify the objective or the goal. Economic thinking, as I've said, is not much help here; it's going to be more helpful when we go to the second, third, and fourth steps. The second stage in making a rational decision, once you know the objective, is to identify all possible alternative paths to help you get there. If you don't know your options, it's hard to systematically choose the best one. The third step is then to evaluate carefully the payoffs from each of those alternatives; and that's where economic thinking can help a lot. We're going to develop some tools through the course of these lectures that will help you with understanding how to put some value on some difficult things. Finally, you have to actually, of course, select the best one and implement your decision. To determine the best course and then willfully choose another one would be to act irrationally; and economists don't like it when people do that.

You remember that in our world of scarcity—the world of the Six Principles—evaluating alternatives is all about valuing the opportunity costs. What is not chosen is the real cost of what you do choose. The cost of any choice is really the value of what you gave up, the choice that was not taken. Rationality says that you should always choose the option with the highest net payoff; to knowingly choose anything worse, that would be irrational. Again, in teenager's language that would be kind of a "duh" conclusion; but it's a very powerful and very valuable predictor of behavior, that concept of rationality.

The presumption of rationality works two ways, of course: It helps us with the prediction and the description of behavior, but it also gives us a way to evaluate ex post—after the fact—to draw some conclusions about values. If I observe you choosing one alternative over another, and believing as I do in rationality, I think you have thereby revealed to me your "true preference"; I know what you value. I may not agree with your preference; that doesn't matter. Clearly you valued it; you valued the chosen alternative over the other options. Thus, because I perceive the world in rationality terms, I know that those ice fishermen value the afternoon on the frozen lake more highly than any other option. They could have spent the afternoon under a cozy quilt sipping herbal tea, but they freely chose instead to sit out there on that frozen lake. That "proves" to me that it was, in their evaluation, the best attainable alternative. For them, that was a rational choice. For my wife to make that choice would be unimaginably insane, and I have every confidence in the world she will never do that. This concept of strategic decision-making and rationality as both an objective for and a description of human behavior is fundamental to economic thinking; it's the first of our Core Concepts.

I'm going to tell you flat out: Economists are marginal thinkers. But that doesn't mean what you think it means; that's not a comment about the quality of their thought, it's a comment about the focus of their thought. Economists tend to look carefully at sequences of small changes made "on the margin," because most of the choices we make in life are not "all or nothing" decisions; most of them are how many more or how much less decisions. In opportunity cost terms, most of our choices involve marginal "trade-offs": A little more of this inevitably means a little bit less of that."

I recently saw a bumper sticker—and you're going to be struck through the course that I often seem to find economic principles in bumper stickers, letters to the editor, and other strange places; but I guess that's a mark of thinking like an economist—and the bumper sticker I saw said, "Housing is a right, not a privilege." The empathetic human in me said, "How true, how true"; but the economist in me said, "That bumper sticker makes no sense." Why not? It doesn't make sense until we specify how much housing each of us has a right to. Do we have a right to a refrigerator box? To a 1,000 square foot bungalow? To a 20,000 square foot mansion with a pool and a tennis court? How much health care, or education, or Caribbean vacations must be foregone to provide it; what would be the opportunity cost? When does having a little more housing reach the line of meeting the right; when is it enough; and when does it cross the line into too much? In a moment, we'll talk about those principles somewhat; but first I want to have fun with a little puzzle that's solvable by marginal thinking. Watch closely as I do this because you can amaze your friends and you'll be able to illustrate the fundamental process of marginal analysis.

Imagine with me: You have a salt shaker, you have a pepper shaker. For reasons that totally escape me, you decide you're going to dip a teaspoon into the pepper shaker, take it over, dump it in the salt shaker, put the lid on, and shake it up; so now I have a teaspoon of pepper in with a mostly salt. I don't know why I want to do this, but suppose now I take the same teaspoon, I dip it into the one that has a lot of salt and a little bit of pepper, I come over, and I dump it into the pepper shaker and shake that one up. Here's the puzzle: After I'm done, is there more pepper in the salt shaker or more salt in the pepper shaker? It sounds tricky, doesn't it? But the answer is simple: The answer is no; there's not more in either one. With marginal analysis I think it's going to be easy to see that the amount of the "added" spice is going to be exactly the same in both situations.

The key to doing that is not to focus on the shakers but to focus on the teaspoons: Follow the sequence of changes in order to understand the effects on the total. Watch the first move: Here's the teaspoon; it's going into the pepper, it's coming out, and there's one teaspoon of pepper in it, and that's the amount that I dump into the salt. That was easy; now it gets more interesting. The second time I do this, and I dip the teaspoon in, it's going to come out mostly salt mixed with a little bit of pepper. How much? $\frac{1}{4}$ teaspoon, 1/16, 1/234; I have no idea. But let's call it x teaspoons of pepper. So x teaspoons of pepper have come out of the salt shaker; how much is left? $1 - x$. Watch the spoon as it's moving toward the other shaker. If x teaspoon is the amount of pepper that's in this teaspoon, how much salt must be in it? The answer, of course, is $1 - x$. It's mostly salt, but it also contains x teaspoons; and when I add that over here, each container ends up with exactly with $1 - x$ teaspoons of the other, no matter what the value of x. By focusing our attention on a sequence of changes, the outcome for the whole becomes crystal clear. We solved this using marginal analysis. The end result for the total is always determined by the changes "on the margin." Marginal analysis is key to many economic insights.

This can be applied in many contexts. For example, I know you've all seen this during a campaign: There's a TV screen; there's an evil-looking mug shot of a convicted, violent criminal; and a voiceover says, "Last year crime cost our city $500 million, yet the incumbent mayor budgeted a mere $75 million for the police." What's the implication? Obviously, the mayor is spending far too little on crime; or is he? An economist will say that statement tells us nothing of value. Yes, it's true: The total cost of crime ($500 million) is greater than the amount spent to fight crime ($75 million); but those numbers measure what's happening in the "shakers." The wisdom of increasing the police budget depends on the teaspoons—on the changes—not on the shakers, which are just the current totals.

Think like an economist for a moment about the statement that was in that television ad. Yes, the total costs of crime are $575 million: $500 million direct costs, $75 million prevention costs. But a change is justified only if it reduces that total, and you evaluate that by looking at the teaspoons, at the changes, at the effects on total of increasing or decreasing the amount that's budgeted. If a marginal, an additional, $1 million is spent for the police but it reduces crime by a mere $100,000, then the marginal gain, the teaspoon, is less than the marginal cost, and the total cost of crime is actually increasing, not decreasing. Only if an additional spending is going to reduce the total cost of crime by more than $1 million—$2.5 million, say—then the expenditure would make sense. The key point from this is the wisdom of any change in policy, or any change in behavior, can only be determined by looking at its net impacts on the margin. Comparing totals tells you very little indeed; understand that, and you're thinking like an economist.

There's one more important aspect: The marginal value of anything is not fixed; it changes as we have more or less of it. Ever since economists became marginal thinkers in the 19th century, that postulate has given them answers to problems that had confounded classical economists for generations. One of those puzzles is what was called the water/diamond paradox; and the question was: Why would rational people pay so much for something so unnecessary like a diamond? Why would people willingly sell so cheaply something that should be so very dear, without which life is impossible: water? With marginal analysis, the way out of this conundrum was obvious, because they shifted attention from the salt shakers to the teaspoons: It's never how much water is worth in the abstract, it's always how much is one more pint of water worth? Of course, that depends on how much you already have.

You've all seen the cliché cartoon: There's a traveler crawling across the harsh desert, there are impatient vultures circling overhead; he's completely without water and life itself is in the balance. If I ask you, "What would be the increase in his welfare from the first pint of water?" the answer is, "That would be incalculable." The single pint, that marginal point, would easily be worth a whole bag of diamonds to that thirst-stricken traveler at that moment. The second would be almost as valuable. But at some point, the gain from one more marginal pint of water becomes less and less, and we say that diminishing returns on the margin have set in. Additional pints are still adding to welfare, they're just not adding as much as they did before. Welfare is rising at a decreasing rate; it's up, but by less and less. The marginal value can become negative; if there was a thunderstorm and a desert flash flood, the traveler would be better off with less water. But the point is that value is always marginal and always situational. That's hard to grasp, but it's an important and powerful concept.

We can apply it in lots of different contexts. For example, if you're a runner and you make a commitment, your resolution, that you're going to shave 30 seconds off your time for the mile, how "expensive" that's going to be probably depends on what your personal best currently is. It will probably take less effort to get a 30-second improvement if your best time is 20 minutes. It'll take quite a bit more if your best time is 7 minutes, and the cost of achieving that may be infinite and impossible if it's 5 minutes. The marginal cost of a 30 second improvement increases as the current record is lowered; the total time keeps falling, but the marginal cost of achieving each improvement keeps rising.

Let's have a pop quiz. One of the courses I teach is an urban economics course; not long ago, I asked some students a question, I want to see how you would answer it. The question was: If we woke up tomorrow and gas prices in the U.S. had doubled, how would that affect automobile usage? One student started with an assertion, "At that price, no one would ever drive their car." That's a bad start for an economics class—not that good a start for an English class since "no one" is singular and "their" is plural, but I'm going to overlook that for a moment—because the question about driving is not an "all or nothing" decision; it's a "more or less" decision, and how much more and how much less. At high gas prices, some trips on the margin would not be worth it, but others certainly still would be; and thinking like an economist means we always reject claims that say that a change in price is going to make things stop altogether. You know that even if most people did stop driving, that would mean the freeways would be empty, there would be easy parking everywhere, and surely that should be enough to cover the pain at the pump for some drivers some of the time. Some level of driving still makes sense; it will be less, but it won't be zero. People adjust on the margin until the value of the last trip taken reflects the new, higher costs of driving.

That's two of our principles, our Core Concepts that we want to talk about today. The third one is about optimization in something called the "equimarginal principle." But before going on to the third concept, let's just summarize where we are for a moment. We're economists, so we're thinking about things on the margin. We're looking at strategically rational decisions. We're talking about scarcity and trade-offs, opportunity cost; more of one thing, less of another. As the marginal value changes, more of something makes the marginal value fall; less of something makes the marginal value rise. Given this, what's the best attainable allocation, the best balance, the best optimal outcome, the maximum achievable given the constraints? Can you use these principles we've devised to "optimize?" The answer's "Yes," by using something that economists called the "equimarginal principle"; and that's the last of our three Core Concepts.

I want to approach this doing a thought experiment; and I'm going to bet that intuitively, you're going to apply equimarginal principle. Unselfconsciously, you're going to end up at the optimal solution without really resorting to all the fancy mathematics we use to determine optimum points in economic model. Here we are: Imagine yourself on a new TV reality show. You come with just the clothes on your back; you're flown by helicopter deep into the wilderness; you're given a special number of "chits" that you get to exchange at a special trading post, for items that are going to aid in your survival. Each chit can buy one unit of food or one unit of shelter. The host, before he's flown back to his comfortable and very well-stocked trailer, is going to voice over, "Welcome to Wilderness Camp. Winter is on the way and you have nothing. You must choose wisely how to spend your chits; choose unwisely and you may not survive until spring. You must now decide whether food or shelter is the best choice." Then he gets on his helicopter, he flies away.

But if you think like an economist—or really any rational human being— I'm sure you're going to just immediately reject his fundamental premise. Survival—and I think survival is part of an optimal outcome—is not about either food or shelter; it's about the best attainable combination of the two. What, exactly, is "best?" To gorge on food while freezing to death is not a good strategy; basking in warmth and comfort while starving to death, not a good strategy either. The "optimal" is to find the balance between food and shelter that, of course, will bring the marginal value of each of them to be equal; hence the name the "equimarginal principle." The contribution on the margin is the same for each.

Let's work this through a little bit. Just consider: Foolishly, you've decided to spend all of your chits on shelter and none for food; so you have lots of shelter, no food. That last unit of shelter is probably nice, but the marginal value, the addition that it added to your welfare, is very low indeed. You're pretty well-sheltered, but you're facing starvation. The first meal, because you have no food, would have a very high marginal value. The meal foregone is the opportunity cost of the last bit of shelter, and it's much higher than the benefit. That was an irrational choice. Every time you trade off one less shelter for one more food, there's a huge net gain. You should make that trade in that situation; it will be rational. But it's not always rational to trade shelter for food; why not?

Suppose you started instead with all food and no shelter. Then, because you had so much food, the marginal value of food would be low and the marginal value of shelter would be high. In that situation, rationality would say, "Trade food, which you have a lot of, for shelter." But no matter which end of this bargain you start at, as you give up more and more of the abundant good, its marginal value, though starting low, is ever rising; as you acquire more and more of the scarce good, its marginal value, though starting high, will be ever falling; and when they meet, when they're equal, you've arrived at the optimum combination. You cannot gain even the tiniest amount by trading one for the other. You're at the pinnacle; you've maximized subject to the constraint; you've gotten as much welfare as possible from the allocation you were given. You've "optimized"; you've done it subconsciously by applying the "equimarginal principle."

There you have it: Apply the concepts of rationality, marginality, and constrained optimization in a world proscribed by the Six Foundation Principles and you're thinking like an economist. We can dress this all up in fancy mathematics, we often do; we can use complex econometric models to test empirically hypothesis about the parameters of the functions in the real world, we often do; but the real essence of learning to think like an economist is to be comfortable with this basic toolkit. After we add "Efficiency" next time, you'll have it all.

We have a few minutes left; so what I'd like to do is just talk about a couple of these principles in a couple of interesting contexts, and think like economists about what would be a rational response to incentives in the following real-world situations. Back in the days of the old Soviet Union, they were very concerned about their world image; and one of the things they did in order to incentivize their athletes was to pay them a cash bonus any time one of them set a new world record, even if they were breaking their own world record. Think with me for a moment about what kind of incentives that created. I'm absolutely sure that their athletes were extremely competitive, but I think they were probably responding rationally to that particular bonus that was going to be available. Athletes would want to break any world record they possibly could, but perhaps they had an incentive to break it by as little as possible so it would be easier to break again. Sergey Bubka set the pole vault record for the first time in 1983. Over the next decade, he broke his own outdoor record 16 times and his own indoor record 17 times; and he often broke it by the merest of margins—a centimeter or less—and then he would quit for the day. Instead of pushing to see how high he could make it, he was satisfied with breaking the record. His incentive apparently was not to set the record as high as he possibly could on any given day, but to set it as often as he could. I think an economist would predict that if the size of the bonus had been dependent on the size of the increase in the record height, the history of modern pole vaulting might have been quite different.

No one who's read both Charles Dickens and Ernest Hemingway will ever confuse one with the other. As artists, their styles were reflections of themselves and reflections of the times in which they wrote; and perhaps also, in some small measure at least, they were reflections in the way they were paid. Most of Dickens' novels were serialized, usually in about 20 parts, and he would receive a contract payment every time he filled up 32 pages of printed text. It wasn't exactly paid by the word, but wordiness certainly helped him to stretch his stories out to the full contracted length. Hemingway, of course, got paid by the completed manuscript. There was no financial incentive for him to modify his sparse style of writing. If Hemingway and Dickens had been paid by identical formulae you still would have been able to tell them apart, their styles would have been different, they would have been distinct; but it doesn't mean that their compensation formula had no impact at all on their writing.

What does this all mean for you? What do you want to take away from this? It means that whether you're writing a book like Hemingway and Dickens; whether you're striving to set a world record like Sergei Bubka; whether you're looking at the compensation formulae for your employees, considering how your financial advisor is paid, or examining the terms of a seasonal contract with your snow plower; thinking like an economist means being ever cognizant of the incentives you face and perhaps more importantly, the incentives those around you face. It means anticipating what's strategically rational for them, and how that will affect your options. It means focusing on the margin, on tradeoffs, and on adjustments to find the optimal balance. The question is always going to be: How much of which?

Next time, we're going to step back just a bit and widen our economic perspective to consider one last concept: the concept of economic efficiency. What is it that economists mean when they use that term? How does it relate to rationality? How does it fit into this paradigm that defines economic thinking? When lots of us as individuals respond strategically to the incentives we personally face, can we be certain that the outcome will be socially efficient? Economists as economists think about that a lot. Next time, so will we.

The Myth of "True Value"
Lecture 3

First and foremost, rational choices can lead all of us involved to better, more socially efficient outcomes. They don't have to. That failing is most likely to take place when our decisions and our strategies are interdependent: When my best strategy depends on your choice; when your best strategy depends on mine. If we don't need each other's consent, if we don't communicate and we don't negotiate, or if some kind of an enforceable agreement isn't possible, we may end up rationally choosing paths that harm us both.

When all of the rational decisions made by individual actors are connected and added up, what are the social consequences? This is the final concept that completes our tool kit: the concept of economic efficiency. Efficiency is related to rationality, but it's slightly different. Rationality refers to the process by which individuals reach choices; efficiency is a measure that we use to judge the social consequences of those many choices. Economists define efficiency as people being made better off. What determines whether you're better off? You do; it's a measure of how you feel.

The more difficult question is when is a society better off? Can we determine objectively when a change is a clear social gain, as opposed to a purely personal gain? Economists spent decades trying to find a good, objective measure of social welfare. Finally, at the beginning of the 20th century, they gave up. They figured they could not find a strong, objective measure of social welfare, so they settled for a very weak one instead. They adopted a principle from the sociologist Vilfredo Pareto, who said that the only unambiguous standard of a social gain is this: If we take a number of people, and something makes any one of them better off by their own judgment without making anyone else worse off, that is an unambiguous social improvement. We call such a situation in which no one can be made better off without harming another a Pareto optimum. The allocation of resources is efficient—not just, not necessarily fair, not philosophically ideal, just efficient. Failure to take advantage of a Pareto improvement would also be inefficient.

When do rational decision processes inevitably lead to Pareto efficient results? Won't there be constant competition for resources? Don't all interactions violate Pareto's standards: One wins, one loses? Whenever there are counterparties, there are conflicting interests. Won't there always be competition to see who will prevail; every sale is a purchase, every loan made is a debt due? In fact, in most of the world, most of the time, there is a significant degree of cooperation and stability. How can that be? Thinking like an economist provides an answer. Economists believe that nothing has a timeless, objective true value. Value to any person is the marginal contribution to that person's welfare, and it can be quite different in different circumstances or for different people. The value of a glass of water when I'm sitting at home next to a free-flowing tap versus when I'm crawling across a broiling desert is quite different. If rationality holds, then no one will pay more for an item than it is worth to them at that time in that circumstance, nor sell it for less, but the 2 parties can be trading a single thing that literally has 2 different values.

The value of a glass of water when I'm sitting at home next to a free-flowing tap versus when I'm crawling across a broiling desert is quite different.

Economic efficiency is the exhaustion of all possible unambiguous increases in self-defined welfare. We know that individual rationality will promote it, as long as the incentives driving each decider reflect the costs and benefits that result from decisions. Each harm must be accurately compensated, each gain must be appropriately priced, rights must be clearly defined, information must be complete and true, and promises must be kept. But this, of course, is not the world in which we live. Our world falls short in so many ways: We may not understand the true consequences of our actions; we may voluntarily choose ones that make us worse off; people may lie about their intentions or break their promises; rights may be ambiguous. It is when the incentives that guide choices fail to be accurate or comprehensive that individual rational choices can make the decider, or someone else, worse off. Thinking like an economist has its greatest value in these instances—by understanding the harms that these imperfections cause and formulating strategies to overcome them. The rest of this course focuses on doing just that. ∎

The Prisoner's Dilemma

The prisoner's dilemma is a problem loved by economists and game theorists. It has implications for us as individuals making decisions, as well as in terms of our survival as a species. Imagine this scenario: The police have arrested 2 suspects and put them in separate interview rooms. They offer each suspect a choice. The suspects cannot communicate with each other, but the choice each makes will affect the other.

Here's the situation: They were arrested for possession of a stolen car, for which they can receive 2-year sentences. But the police also believe the car was used in a drive-by shooting, and to get that conviction, they need a confession from at least 1 suspect—this will give them the charge of assault with a deadly weapon. The police tell each suspect that if he testifies against the other, he'll get a 1-year sentence for the auto theft and a walk on the shooting. The second suspect will take the fall; he'll do 8 years for the crimes. The prosecutors know, however, that if both testify, they won't need a trial at all, and each person will get a plea bargain sentence of 4 years. If both suspects stonewall, there's only enough evidence to convict them on the stolen car charge, and each will do 2 years.

What's the individual rational decision for each suspect? This is the realm of game theory. Game theorists look for interdependent strategic decisions, putting each individual's best response to a situation into a framework called a payoff matrix. Each player says, "If he does x, what does that do for me if I do a or if I do b?" An example in this case looks like this: If he confesses, and I don't confess, I'll do 8 years; if I also confess, I'll do 4. My conclusion is that if my partner is in the other room confessing, I minimize my cost by confessing myself. But what if my partner doesn't confess? Then if I confess and testify, I'll serve only 1 year; if I stonewall while he's stonewalling also, I'll get 2. One year is better than doing 2 years. So if he does not confess, I minimize my cost by confessing. Regardless of my partner's strategy, the optimal choice for me—the individually rational choice for me—is to confess. Of course, my partner faces the same payoff matrix, so no matter what I do, his best strategy is to confess. As a consequence, both confess and serve 4 years. If they were able to trust each other or communicate, they would each do 2 years.

Of course, the police were thinking like economists. They created this situation so the suspects' incentives did not compel any concern for each other. The police left each suspect to make an individually rational choice—to his own, and their collective, detriment. We encounter prisoner's dilemmas in many contexts. Whenever decisions are interdependent but have to be made individually and there are no enforceable agreements or compensation, it can lead to harmful results.

Take-Away Points

1. Truly voluntary interactions between rational individuals will make all of them better off and will thereby improve social efficiency.

2. However, when rational individual decisions are interdependent and are not the result of negotiated consent and enforceable agreements, rational individual choices can lead to social outcomes detrimental to all parties (as in the prisoner's dilemma).

The Myth of "True Value"
Lecture 3—Transcript

I want to welcome you back to the third lecture in our series on how to think like an economist. Today what I want to do is broaden our focus just a little bit. So far, we've been paying the closest attention to the strategic decision-making that rational individuals will undertake in a world of scarcity. What would or should a rational individual do in different circumstances? That's a question we ask ourselves as participants in the economy. But as economists, we're also concerned with a broader, related question: What happens when lots of rational individuals make decisions that are optimal for themselves; does that always come out to be best for everyone, sometimes, often, always, never? That's really the question that economists as professionals are most often addressing: How does a society fare when it's made up of rational, individual decision makers? That's going to bring us to one final concept today: the concept of economic efficiency.

Efficiency is related to rationality, but it's a little bit different: Rationality is looking at the process by which individuals reach their decisions; efficiency is measuring the consequences of all those many choices. What we're going to do first today: We're going to define efficiency the way economists do, and then we're going to try to develop our ability to use that in context. The second thing we'll do is take a first cut at trying to figure out the conditions that have to be fulfilled if rational individual choices are going to result in efficient social outcomes. Then, finally, we'll take a look at this one classic situation that's called the prisoner's dilemma. It's a case where rational individual decisions lead to an inefficient outcome: what people choose to do rationally turns out to be less than the best for themselves and less than the best for society. We'll revisit that kind of problem later in other lectures. I just want to emphasize that those are the situations where thinking like an economist is going to be the most valuable. There's not much urgency in rushing to the doctor for advice when you're completely healthy; and similarly, there's not that much need of thinking like an economist when everything is running perfectly smoothly. It's when we're faced with imperfections and obstacles, when there are problems in the way, that economic thinking becomes the most valuable.

Let's start talking about the definition of efficiency for an economist. Efficiency, like rationality, means different things in different contexts. If you ask an engineer what's efficient, she'll tell you, "It's achieving a given amount of work with a minimum amount of energy." If you ask an economist what's efficiency, the economist can say, "It's defined in terms of making people as well-off as they can be given the resources available." Who determines when you're well off; who determines when you're better off? An economist doesn't; you do. Just as rationality makes no judgments about the wisdom of the objectives, efficiency's not about whether you should feel better off, it really is going to ask only if you do. If you honestly consider yourself better off sitting out on the ice for an hour, looking at that hole hoping a fish will bite, then ice fishing does make you better off. It's a rational choice to do it; it's an efficient outcome having done it, no matter what my wife thinks about the process. I get to decide what's best for me; you get to decide what's best for you; and then, if we're both rational, we each will have picked our own best option. That's settled.

There's a harder question, though: When are things best for us? When is a society made better off when there are lots of people involved; how do you judge that? When is a change a clear social, as opposed to just an individual or personal, gain? Economists have struggled with that question for decades, trying to figure out when one social outcome is better than another social outcome. By the time they got to the mid-20th century, they resolved the conflict by frankly just giving up. They decided that they could never find a strong objective measure of social welfare, so we've settled for a pretty weak one instead. Economic efficiency is based on a principle first proposed by a sociologist named Vilfredo Pareto; and he argued that the only unambiguous standard for saying "This is a better outcome than that" is: If it makes at least one person better off by their own judgment without making anyone else worse off, then we can say that's an unambiguous social improvement. A Pareto Optimum, then, is when we've reached a place where no one can be made any better off without making someone else worse off. For an economist, when you reach Pareto Optimum, that's efficient; no unambiguous gains remain to be satisfied. It doesn't mean it's just, it doesn't mean it's fair, it doesn't mean it's philosophically ideal; it just means it's efficient.

Failure to take advantage of a Pareto improvement also would be inefficient. Rationality and efficiency are pretty closely linked; and the distinction between them is subtle but it's important if you're going to understand how to think like an economist: Rationality describes the process of making wise individual choices; efficiency is evaluating the social consequences. When do rational individual decisions made here lead to efficient results over here?

If you think about our foundation principles, it sounds like they're a prescription for perpetual and bitter conflict. This is a world of scarcity; there is always a cost, at least in opportunity terms. Doesn't that mean that there has to be a constant competition for resources? Doesn't that mean that the resources one person used cannot be used by another? Doesn't that mean that one person's gain is always going to come at another's expense? Doesn't that mean all interactions violate Pareto's standards? After all, there are always "counterparties"—every sale is a purchase, every loan is a debt due—and the consequence of all that feels like it could be what Thomas Hobbes characterized as "war of one against all where life is nasty, brutish, and short." There are some failed states where Hobbes's vision seems to hold true; but in most of the world, most of the time, we seem to have a significant degree of cooperation and stability. How can that be? Thinking like an economist, I think, is going to provide an answer.

I once came across two friends who were having a fairly heated argument, and one of them was arguing that in any transaction, one party is always taking advantage of the other; they can't both win because they're trading the same thing. Shopping, she argued, was like hunting: one must be predator, one must be prey. Either the buyer tricks the seller into accepting less than true value, or the seller has to trick the buyer into paying more than true value. But thinking like an economist, you see the transaction differently. Do you remember when we talked last time about the diamond/water paradox? The economist argues that nothing has a real, intrinsic, timeless true value; the value to anybody is the marginal contribution it's going to make to that person's welfare, and the contribution can be quite different in different circumstances. The value of a glass of water when I'm sitting at home next to a free-flowing tap is very different than the value of that same glass of water if I'm crawling across a parched desert. If rationality holds, then no one is going to willingly pay more for an item than it is worth to them, or sell it for less than it is worth to them; so that in any well-informed, voluntary exchange both parties can win because they are literally trading one thing that has two different values.

Here's an example: Suppose that somehow I came into possession of a ticket to a concert by the latest teenage heartthrob band. I can assure you I'm probably better off by trading that ticket for virtually anything—something trivial, a bagel—because attending that concert for two hours would be pure vexation to me; but it could be as dear as life to a young friend of mine. If we were to trade, both of us would be made better off by that transaction: I could sit happy at home with my bagel, and she could be thrilled beyond words to be attending the concert of her dreams. No predator, no prey; a contented, well-fed economist and an ecstatic teen. That's a win-win situation that's a whole lot better than my spending the evening at the concert with my fingers in my ears while she sits at home, crying tears onto her unwanted bagel. Value in transactions has to be judged on the margin from the perspectives of the potential participants. In a voluntary exchange, both parties can and do benefit. It's true for bagels and boy bands, and it's true for travelers and profit-maximizing airlines as well.

Every week, I get emails at the last minute. I got one not long ago from an airline that said, "Fly to Las Vegas tomorrow, be back for work on Monday, only $49 each way." $49? That's not even going to begin to cover the cost per seat of flying that big jet all the way across the country. Clearly the airline is losing something here; the airline must be the prey. But you know that's not true; there really aren't losers in that deal if you think like an economist about it and you focus on the margin, you focus on the impact, of a series of small changes. Come Friday afternoon, that seat is going to fly across the country; the question the airline faces is: Will there be a paying passenger sitting in it? By Thursday night, everyone for whom the value of the trip that Friday is worth at least the normal fee—say $456—they've already purchased a nonrefundable ticket. That was a voluntary transaction; and the voluntary transaction meant that the passenger put "cash on the barrelhead," which was a clear revelation: that trip at that price was making them better off. Then the question is: Is there another transaction that can make anyone better off and no one worse off? The plane's going; the marginal cost of putting another passenger into that plane is virtually zero; so any increase in revenue—even the skimpy $49—is greater than the cost, the marginal cost, of flying that passenger. The airline's better off than flying empty seats; the bargain passengers are better off than staying home; and even the full-fare passengers are better off than they would have been had they stayed home. I suppose the full-fare passengers might wish that they'd waited for last-minute bargain tickets, and they could have won even more; but that's not the same thing as saying that they were actually losing.

Rational individuals would and presumably will voluntarily enter into any transaction that makes them better off; and if all the participants are made better off, it's a Pareto improvement, it increases efficiency. That's really the basis for Adam Smith's famous observation in his book *The Wealth of Nations* that he published in 1776. In that book he argued that the most selfish person who engages in a voluntary exchange is guided "by an invisible hand to promote an end which was no part of his intention." That central conclusion—that in any freely-entered-into transactions all parties get made better off—is really why economists have such [affinity] for markets; they like markets because markets promote efficiency. That's really why, given our foundation principle that no one is in control, things really work out. I'm always astonished when I walk into a supermarket and the shelves are covered with food. Some farmer somewhere in Kansas put forth extraordinary effort to grow wheat and deliver it to a flour mill. Some miller put forth great effort to grind it up and turn it into flour; some baker baked it, turned it into bread; and a teamster drove across country to deliver it to me. None of them know me; none of them care much about me. While it seems as if they were doing all of this for me, in truth they did it all for themselves; it was pursuit of their gain that motivated them to meet my need. I am fed; they are paid; all of us are better off. Rational choices increase social efficiency.

If it works once, why not time and again? Wouldn't it be rational to just keep searching out more and more and more gains until there's absolutely no potential gain left? Do you remember when we started this course and I said if you adopt an economist's paradigm it's going to shape everything you see for the rest of your life? one night last week, late in the evening, I was having trouble sleeping so I got up and turned on the TV, and I happened to come upon a nature documentary on something called a star-nosed mole. This is an extraordinary creature; it has 22 tentacle-like projections that come right out of the end of its nose, and as it burrows underground those tentacles are constantly sampling and seeking everything that it comes in contact with, looking for any opportunity for gain. It takes immediate advantage of that and moves on to the next. You know what my distorted response was to this? My first thought was, "Metaphorically, that is the truly rational decision maker, constantly seeking out any improvement in position, taking full advantage of it until all potential gains are realized and captured." Rational deciders won't consent to their own harm; they won't refuse a clear game. Rational individuals won't walk away and leave "money on the table."

That's the basis of an old joke about an economist and a political scientist; it goes like this: An economist and a political scientist are walking down the street. The political scientist says, "Look, there's a $20 bill on the ground," and the economist responds, "There can't be. If there were, someone would have picked it up already." You're not laughing; it doesn't seem that funny. But if you tell that joke to a bunch of economists, they'll be giggling uncontrollably. It's a strange phenomenon, but it captures how economists see the world.

Let me take a moment and summarize and emphasize: At the participant level, thinking like an economist means focusing your attention on the rationality of individual choices. On the professional level, thinking like an economist means focusing your attention on the efficiency of results. When all the potential unambiguous increases and self-defined welfare have been captured, then we are efficient. When some remain, or when harms result, we're inefficient. The economist's professional concern is with inefficiency.

Our second question today is: What's necessary to make rational individual choices result in socially efficient outcome? In a nutshell, it's just this: the actual incentives that they face must be true, complete, and accurate. Every single harm incurred must be compensated for; every gain experienced must be appropriately priced; the rights that people have must be clearly defined; the information upon which we base our decisions must be complete and true; the bargained promises we make must be kept; and if we do all that, there's probably not much need to think like an economist, because the "invisible hand" seems to be working fine. But what if there's some distortion, some inaccuracy, some failing so that the incentives that are guiding our choices are somehow wrong? The decisions we make, then, can be harmful to ourselves; we can voluntarily choose outcomes that make us, or someone else, worse off. If the incentives that guide our choices are not comprehensive and accurate, then this link between rational decisions and efficient outcomes is broken; rationality and efficiency fail as perfect mirror images of each other. Here's where thinking like an economist is the most valuable: If we can understand what's causing the difficulties, if we can figure out ways to address the consequences of them, then we can adopt strategies to overcome or correct them and we can, again, make rationality result in efficiency. Most of the rest of the course we're going to spend doing just that.

Today what I want to do, for the rest of this lecture, is talk about one such case—and it's kind of an esoteric problem—but we're going to encounter it in lots of different contexts, and it has implications for our decisions as individuals, and perhaps even for our survival as a species (but more on that later). What I want you to do now is imagine a scene; it's one you've seen countless times on police dramas on TV: Two suspects have been arrested and the police have put them in separate interview rooms. A detective goes into each room and offers each of them a choice. The choice is going to affect them both, but they're not allowed to communicate with each other. Here's the situation: They were arrested while driving in a stolen car, and the prosecutor's planning to take a two-year sentence for possession of a stolen car, and they have ample evidence in order to convict on that. But the police also believe that the two suspects were involved in a drive-by shooting earlier that night, but they don't have enough evidence; so they need a confession and perhaps even the testimony of one to convict the other of this serious assault with a deadly weapon charge. They go in and they offer a deal: "Testify against the other man and I'll offer you a one-year sentence for the auto theft and a walk on the shooting. He'll take the fall, a hard eight years for the combined crimes; help yourself out, now's the time, confess."

Of course, the other suspect is being offered exactly the same deal; and so you're suspicious that if he flips first, you're the one who's going to do the full eight years. It turns out that if both of you confess right away, the prosecutors don't need either of you, so they don't need somebody to testify, but they don't want to pay for two trials; so if both confess, they'll settle for a plea bargain sentence of four years each. If you both hold the line, if you both stonewall, they only have enough evidence to convict on the stolen car charge, and each does two years. The question is: What's the individually rational decision for each of these suspects? If you're going to think like an economist about this, you're going to find yourself deep into something called game theory. Game theorists try to look at situations where players have independent strategic decisions, and they're going to put the effects of that into something called a payoff matrix. In looking at the other player's possible moves and anticipating the consequences for yourself, each player is supposed to determine an optimal strategy if they possibly can.

Here's how we would structure this: We'd have a table with four cells in it, and we'd put the possibilities for my opponent on top; and so we'd say, "If the opponent confesses, or the opponent does not confess"; and then down the side we'll put my options—"I confess, I do not confess"—and then in each of the boxes we'll have the consequences for me. Let's look at it: If he confesses and I confess, we'll both do four years' time. If he confesses and I do not confess, my sentence is going to be eight years. If he's down the hall confessing, I minimize my sentence by confessing as well. If, on the other hand, he's down the hall holding the line, refusing to confess, and I do confess, I'm only going to have a sentence of one year. But if he holds the line and I hold the line, I'll do two years. If he's down the hall holding the line, stonewalling, refusing to confess, I minimize my sentence by confessing. What's the conclusion? If he confesses, I should also. If he does not confess, my best strategy is to confess. Regardless of his strategy, my best choice—the individually rational choice for me—is to go ahead and confess. Of course, he faces the same payoff matrix, he's doing the same thing; and so as a consequence what we're going to find is that both of us confess, both of us end up doing four years. That was the rational decision for each of us individually, but had we stonewalled, we each would have done two. We made rational individual choices that combined into an outcome that was less than best for both of us. Why? Mostly because we could not communicate; we dared not trust; we could not form an enforceable agreement.

Who was thinking like an economist in this particular situation? The answer, of course, is the police; they purposefully shaped the incentives to make sure that the rational decisions made by the suspects would benefit the police's position. They laid a rationality trap. Neither suspect had much incentive to consider the costs his decision imposed on the other; he didn't have to pay compensation for harm; he didn't get paid for a benefit he conferred; he didn't have to get the consent of his confederate in the whole thing; they couldn't negotiate, communicate, or have an enforceable agreement. The police created incentives for the suspects so that they would both make individually rational decisions to their collective detriment.

We're going to encounter prisoner's dilemmas in several different contexts. Whenever our decisions are independent but are made individually, and we don't have enforceable agreements and we can't require compensation, rational choices can lead to collectively harmful results. Here's an example close to home: My youngest son wrestled all through high school and college, and each week he was faced with a difficult choice. In order to wrestle, you must "make weight," and often wrestlers trying to seek an advantage will go to great lengths to cut weight: starving themselves; putting on rubber suits and running around so they sweat off all kinds of water; some have even been known to have some of their blood withdrawn, get weighed, and have the blood put back in just to get those last few ounces. That can be damaging to their health, and there have even been examples of wrestlers who died trying to cut weight with extreme efforts of dehydration and other health difficulties, just so you can be bigger and stronger than your opponent.

That's a smart strategy perhaps, unless your opponent's doing the same thing; and if he is, at match time, two 170-pound wrestlers, both of whom risked their health, temporarily reduced their weight below 160, and they end up wrestling each other anyway. If both of them could be sure that their opponent was not cutting weight, they could wrestle each other without the risk to their health. But neither one of them, making a rational individual choice, dared not to cut weight, because they might end up, then, wrestling a 185-pounder who was able to squeeze his weight down to 170. They were caught in a difficult prisoner's dilemma, and there's no easy solution to that. Individually rational decisions were making both wrestlers worse off. The only way this was ever solved was to change the underlying payoffs that came from cutting weight; and the wrestlers alone—like the suspects locked up in the police station—really had no ability to do that themselves. How that was finally solved was that following a series of deaths from cutting weight, the governing sports organization came in and brought in some external authority and changed the payoffs. At the beginning of each season, they do a physical exam on wrestlers and give them a minimum certified weight that said they may not legally wrestle below that weight; there's no advantage to be gained by cutting below the minimum, and only then were rational individual choices made consistent with mutually beneficial results. Sometimes it takes a third party to make rational choices become efficient.

It's not just robbers and wrestlers who get trapped by this. Not long ago, two of the major producers of canned soup got into an advertising war. Each one was arguing about the healthful, good, natural qualities of its own ingredients, and making allegations about unhealthful, unorganic, perhaps dangerous additives in the other's soup. Once they'd begun down that path, they were both trapped; they were in a prisoner's dilemma, because if one company voluntarily quit, the competitor's best option would be to continue the negative advertising and push it as far as they possibly could. If the other company continues, the competitor has no choice but to continue as well in an arms race of advertising charges. Can you predict the outcome? Both of them did continue; the negative comparisons continued to be part of the ads. The net result? The sales of all canned soup declined; consumers apparently came to distrust the whole product line. Had those companies never started down the path, they would have had higher sales and lower advertising budgets; but once they were in, there was no clear way out. They could not meet, perhaps, and agree to stop doing it without running afoul of antitrust laws, and if they did that there'd be a different kind of prisoner's dilemma that they might have to find. They had trapped themselves.

What can we learn from all of this? What are the take away points? First and foremost, rational choices can lead all involved to better, more socially efficient outcomes, but they don't have to; and the failing comes most often when our decisions and the strategies we use are interdependent: when my best strategy depends on your choice, and your best strategy depends on mine. But we do not need each other's consent before we make our choices; if we cannot or do not communicate and negotiate, if enforceable agreements are not possible, we may rationally choose paths that are going to harm us both. Prisoner's dilemmas are everywhere. We're going to encounter them again.

Fortunately, economic thinking, I think, may provide a way out of this. In the next lecture, what we're going to do is take our analysis of the prisoner's dilemma out onto the high seas and we're going to take a look at one of a very serious number of pressing environmental problems of our time. We're going to see how it's economists who devised a solution to "free" some of these prisoners, and we'll take an opportunity to see how that solution is working out.

Incentives and Optimal Choice
Lecture 4

Each time we establish a right or a rule, we're defining incentives and we're affecting other people's behavior.

So far in this course, we have built our economic thinking tool kit and used it to explore a central conclusion in economics: Individuals making rational choices can aggregate into socially efficient outcomes. But in some cases, individual choices can end up making everyone worse off. This lecture explores the issues of incentives and optimal choice as illustrated by the prisoner's dilemma being played out today on the high seas.

Several of the world's commercial fisheries are on the verge of collapse; overfishing has been depleting the populations, and the rate of catch has become unsustainable. In the game theoretic context, commercial fishers are the prisoners, because what it makes sense for each of them to do individually is leading to a disaster for all of them collectively. All of the fishers could get together and agree to catch less, but large agreements like that are almost impossible to negotiate and invariably break down. Under the current payoff matrix, if everyone else restricts their fishing, I'm best off taking as much as I can. If no one else restricts their fishing, I'm still best off taking all that I can. Current controls have proven inadequate: There is a limit on the length of the season, which gets shortened each year in order to limit the total catch. But fish populations continue to decrease, so the season must get shorter, and the incentives for individual fishers become extreme. They buy bigger and faster boats and more expensive equipment; and they go out regardless of weather conditions, making fishing increasingly dangerous.

Something has to be done. An economist came up with a very basic solution, which was first put into practice in Iceland. The thinking is that changing individual incentives changes behavior, which changes the social outcome. Incentives were redesigned so that the behavior of individual fishers would become more consistent with the preservation of fisheries, rather than their eventual destruction. Each fishery is assigned a total allowable catch for the year, and each boat is then assigned an individual tradable quota. The

Tradable quotas are helping to combat the problem of overfishing.

fishing seasons are expanded, decreasing the incentive to fish in dangerous conditions. And there's even more economics to this: The quotas are not only permanent, they are also tradable. Now a superior boat can increase its catch—if it buys shares from someone else. A boat with problems, or even a lazy captain, can avoid the danger and the cost of putting to sea. Both parties in a voluntary trade of rights are made better off; it is Pareto efficient. Overfishing is controlled, and the prisoner's dilemma is solved.

The issue of overfishing teaches us to examine rules and rights. In some cases, rights are determined for the players by an outside force, such as the government. In other situations, the rules have evolved as part of a game, designed and accepted by the players themselves. Defining rights can remove obstacles to Pareto efficient outcomes and trades; in fact, the implicit wisdom in economic thinking has become a foundation for principles of law. What does all of this mean for you? It means that in thinking like an economist, you should always ask yourself the following questions: Are the rules and rights in this situation creating any prisoner's dilemma incentives— incentives that cause individuals to adopt rational strategies that ultimately harm us all? Could the rules or rights be redesigned or renegotiated to induce individuals to reach better decisions? Rights and rules define incentives and optimal individual strategies. Anticipating how is a large part of thinking like an economist. ∎

Take-Away Points

1. The rules and rights surrounding any interaction define the incentives that relevant individuals face. Altering, clarifying, or redefining rights will also redefine optimal strategies for players.

2. Rights and rules can be consciously designed for the purpose of influencing the choices and behavior of others. Examples in this lecture are ownership of any residual after college textbooks are bought or tradable rights to a share of commercial fishing catch.

Incentives and Optimal Choice
Lecture 4—Transcript

I want to welcome you back for the fourth lecture in this series on how to think like an economist. The last time, we came upon for the very first time a peculiar situation where individuals were making rational choices, but it ended up making them all worse off in the end. Today what I want to do is extend that thinking a little bit and focus on some of the ways in which rules and rights create incentives that can make rational decision-makers make more intelligent decisions. I want to start out with a story from the high seas.

Scientists and fishers agree: The world's fisheries are on the verge of collapse. Overfishing is depleting the populations of fish, and at the rate at which we're catching them, those catches are unsustainable. At this pace, virtually all of the commercial fishers in the world are going to be out of business in a few decades, and one of the premier sources of protein for growing human populations will be gone. You don't have to be an economist to conclude that it's a very undesirable outcome. But if everyone sees that overfishing is going on, why does overfishing continue unabated? For economists, the answer is: This is the prisoner's dilemma, but it's being played out on the open ocean. Commercial fishers are the prisoners, at least in a game theoretic context. What it makes sense for each of them to do individually is really creating a disaster for all of them and probably for all of us down the road as well.

I suppose theoretically all the fishers could get together and they could agree that they'd catch less. Long term that would make them all better off; but agreements like that, with thousands of participants, are really impossible to negotiate, they've very, very difficult to enforce, and invariably they break down. If you consider the idea of a payoff matrix that we talked about last time, the payoff matrix for each boat: If everyone else is restricting their catch, them my best option is to take as much as I really can, because my large catch will have no real harm on the environment but a substantial gain for myself; and if no one else is restricting, then there's really no environmental benefit to my holding back. I'd best take all I can, while I can. There's not really any kind of a voluntary agreement among thousands of fishers that's going to be able to withstand that kind of an individual calculus. There's going to have to be some kind of effective limits, some kind of controls put on, that will have to be compulsory and enforceable; but in what kind of a form?

The current controls, the current regulations, have proven wholly inadequate. Here's what happens now: People catch fish; we shorten the legal season in order to limit the total catch; but fish populations keep getting lower and lower. So we make the season shorter and shorter, and that just makes the incentives for individual fishers even more intense. By now it's gotten to the point that it's sort of like the [1889] Oklahoma land rush. Remember in that case they opened land in Oklahoma to settlement, the authorities fired a starting pistol, and people raced in a mad scramble across the countryside to be the first one to get to the best land. Cheaters, of course, came in "sooner" than the rest and created a nickname for Oklahomans even today. But in the ocean version, there's this frantic "race to fish"; when the season opens, you have to get to the fish fastest, take as much as you possibly can, and do it in the absolute shortest time.

What incentives does that create? It says buy a faster boat, buy more gear, get more expensive electronics so that you can catch more and more fish in a shorter and shorter amount of time, it says go out no matter how dangerous the weather; and the result? More and more efficient boats fishing ever more intensively in dangerous conditions that still catch so much that the population remains threatened. So next year, we have to shorten the season once again, and all the boats are stuck in that game theory prison. By the mid-1990s, the season for Alaskan halibut was down to three days out of the entire year, and yet the population still remained threatened; and worse than that, because all the boats went fishing at the exact the same time and returned at the end of those three days, there'd be a temporary glut. The price of halibut would go down; the cost and the danger of fishing was up, the price of fishing was down, the fishery was near collapse. Each boat was acting rationally, and in the process they were destroying their collective livelihood.

Something has to be done; and who are you going to call in a crisis like that? Obviously, an economist. Economists would tell you that the way to address this is to find some way to change the individual incentives, and that will change behavior, and that will change the social outcome. Can you redesign the incentives so the behavior of individual fishers becomes consistent with the preservation of fisheries rather than with their destruction? Iceland was the first place to try this simple economic-thinking solution, and here's how it works: First, biologists determine what is the total allowable catch for the entire fleet, and then they break it into pieces and they assign individual tradable quotas—a right in perpetuity—to a share of the total catch, and they assign that to each boat. For example: If the allowable catch is 100 million pounds, a boat with an individual tradable quota of 1% is entitled to catch of up to 1 million pounds that year. They can fish this week, they can fish next week, they can fish next month; they can wait for good weather, wait for better conditions, or wait for the price to rise. No matter how good the equipment, if it's the best in the fleet, there's no gain from getting to the sea faster than the others, there's no advantage to fishing more fish per hour, because no matter how or when that boat fishes, its catch cannot exceed 1 million pounds; it reaches that level, it's done.

There's another piece to this, and this is where some of the real economics comes in: The right for that boat is permanent; it continues into the future, and it's tradable. If the fish population grows over time, each boat's permitted catch is going to grow with it. If next year the total allowable catch becomes 120 million pounds, that boat with the individual tradable quota is entitled to 1.2 million pounds. But if the allowable catch falls to 80 million pounds, no matter how much effort he puts forth, no matter how much he investments in his equipment, his catch next year will not be allowed to exceed 800,000 pounds. Having the fishery recover now guarantees each boat an individual future gain. Individual rights become more valuable as the fishery recovers. Each captain has a personal incentive to preserve and improve the health of the fishery.

What about the tradability portion of this? That promotes some efficiency in the fleet. Before the quota system, if a boat had mechanical problems, inferior gear, it had a shortage of skilled crew or any other problem, it had a single incentive: go to sea anyway or lose all. Before the quota system, if a boat had superior equipment or crew, it had an incentive to try and catch as many fish as it possibly could, thereby threatening in reality its own and everyone else's future in pursuit of a very short-term gain. With individual tradable rights, a superior boat can still catch more, but only by buying quota. An inferior boat, one with problems or a lazy captain, can sell share and still have some income without risking life and limb out on the high sea. Both parties are made better off by the trade, but that's only possible because they're well-established rights. It's Pareto efficient. Overfishing is controlled, the prisoner's dilemma is solved, the prisoners have been paroled, all because someone had the wisdom to think about this problem like an economist. Defining ownership rights redefined incentives and altered behavior.

After Iceland's success with this, other places have tried it. In Alaska now they're using it for halibut and crab; and the Alaskan halibut season that I said was once down to a very intense, dangerous three days, has now grown back to a full eight months. According to *The Economist* magazine, as a result the total value of the halibut catch has increased by two-thirds, there are 70% fewer emergency search and rescue missions, and there are 15% fewer deaths associated with halibut fishing. This individual tradable quota system is just clear evidence of how having effective rights can make rational individual decisions become efficient and wise social outcomes. In this case, it took someone to consciously step in and redefine these rights for the explicit purpose of redefining incentives.

Sometimes efficient rules just evolve by custom rather than by conscious design. Near my house there is an auto repair shop, and I notice that every morning two panel trucks arrive and they sit in the parking lot for maybe a half an hour or so. The first one offers coffee, donuts, and snacks and it's pretty easy to see why: The mechanics are clearly hungry and thirsty, and they can save time by not having to go out to get their morning coffee break, food and drink come to them; the caterer makes money from the business; the mechanics and the employer save time. It's an efficient solution; all parties are better off. But the second truck that comes and parks there is doing something unusual: It's selling sockets, wrenches, screwdrivers, and other hand tools, but it's selling them to the individual mechanics. When you first look at it that seems a little strange: These are hourly employees, why are they buying the tools? They don't pay for the electricity or the heat; they don't buy the hydraulic lifts or computer diagnostic equipment; the employer typically pays for those. Office workers aren't asked to buy their own pens and printer ink; so how do you explain this peculiar custom of having mechanics but not the employer buy the hand tools? An economist is going to look for the answer to that question in incentives and in efficiency.

Hand tools, of course, are pretty easily lost, misappropriated, misappropriated, or misplaced; and while the cost of each individual socket or ratchet is not that high, the cumulative costs can pretty quickly mount. A key tool that's missing in the middle of a job causes lots of delay, lost production, and higher labor costs. Are there rights or rules that can control the loss of tools at a minimum cost to the employer and make the whole business more efficient? There are different ways you could do this. One possibility was the employer is just going to pay for the tools and provide them. Whenever one is lost, broken, or misplaced, the employer goes out and buys another one. After all, employees are paid by the hour, they don't have a lot of incentive to care carefully for the tools; it doesn't cost them much if the tool is lost or broken. But the employer has to pay the cost of taking constant inventory, and then he has to find out and replace tools that are lost or broken. It's the mechanics who determine the care with which the tools are used, but it's not the mechanics that pay the cost of carelessness. So perhaps an employer will have to find some way to change the mechanics' incentives to make it rational for them to be more careful with what are perhaps his tools.

One possibility: Some factories run a central system where employees check out tools, and at the end of the day they check them in and they're inspected, and then they get docked if the tool is not returned or the tool is misused. But there's a lot of effort and expense incurred in monitoring and enforcing such a system, and particularly so if there's lots of little parts, as there would be in a socket system. The employer has to trade high administrative costs in order to get lower tool costs. Here's another option: Suppose an employer offered a higher wage to mechanics if they would agree to provide their own tools. After all, it's the mechanics that are in a situation where they can reduce the tool loss and damage; and if they're the ones who bear the costs of loss or damage, now they have an incentive to use those tools with extra care. As long as the wage premium is less the employer would have to pay in administrative costs, and it's also more than a careful mechanic would have to pay to keep his tools available and operating, both parties are better off. That's a very common rule that I think has evolved really by practice and custom—I doubt if there was ever a time when they sat down and carefully negotiated that system—but it recognizes the role of incentives; and economists looking at that see it through a lens that says, "That is Pareto efficient." It's efficiency that I think explains why mechanics, carpenters, plumbers, and other tradesmen own their own tools; why in top quality restaurants the chefs own their own knives: It's just one more aspect of how Smith's invisible hand is pointing to an efficient destination.

When you think like an economist, you're going to recognize that rights and rules define incentives, they affect behavior. It's true in the most complex of negotiations, and it can be true in very simple things in everyday life. I have a friend whose daughter recently went to college, and my friend said, "Just send me the bill for your textbooks, I'll pay for them." As happened to all of us who've sent kids off to college, she was utterly stunned when the bill for several hundred dollars for a single semester's books showed up in her mailbox. Brand new texts cost $100 easily; then there are the supplementary readings, etc. The mother, who's an economist, thought about the role of incentives; so next semester, she altered the terms of the deal: She sent her daughter a fixed dollar amount that was quite a bit less than had been spent last semester; but she said to the daughter, "You can keep any residual that's left over after your textbooks are acquired." The rules have been changed. Used books looked much more attractive; library reserves seemed much less burdensome; sharing a text with a friend seemed like a very wise idea. At the end, both she and her mother made money because they had a new set of rules. Rationality isn't just relevant in how you play a game; it's an integral part of designing a game as well. Without clear rights and rules, incentives are ambiguous and confusion reigns; mutually beneficial options remain untaken; money is left on the table. Clearly defined rights mean clear incentives; and then we're able to make rational decisions that are going to allow us to pick up some of that money.

I'm sure all of you at some point came across Robert Frost's famous poem, where one of his neighbors asserted over a rock wall that "good fences make good neighbors," each keeping to his own side. In the modern world, there are lots of conflicts among neighbors that can reach across even well-maintained stone walls. One such example comes from California, where there have been a number of conflicts over sunlight and shade. As energy prices rise and environmental concerns increase, a number of people have been converting to try to use more renewable and fewer fossil fuels. But what if you install an array of photoelectric panels on your roof, and then find that for several hours your neighbor's trees are keeping those panels in deep shadow? Do you have the right to direct sunlight that he's obligated to respect? Does he have the right to plant any trees in his yard he wishes? Does it matter which came first? If we don't have clarity as to the rights, no neighbor has any clarity about their own incentives about the gains and the costs.

California tried to solve this in 1978 by passing a statute called the Solar Shade Control Act. The legislature set certain minimum setbacks, defined what solar collectors were, put maximum heights for shade trees, and tried to define how many hours of shade per day and at what times would constitute interference. After this whole law was passed, it would seem that the issue was statutorily settled. In 1986, there was a case, though, where the owner of a passive solar home asked Santa Clara County to use that statute to require his neighbor to trim or to remove the trees on his lot. The homeowner didn't have active solar collection equipment, what he had was a long exposed southern bank of windows and a large south-facing concrete patio that would serve as a solar heat sink; but the neighbor's trees had reached such a height that by midday they were casting shadow on his passive solar home. What's the answer? Of course, this is America, they went to court; and in the court, the court decided that a passive solar home did not fit into the details of that statutory definition of a solar collector. The neighbor's trees were not, therefore, in violation of the law. Case closed; story over.

Or perhaps not: Now that the lawyers are through, an economist might have something more to say, especially if that economist was named Ronald Coase. Coase won a Nobel Prize in Economics in 1991 mostly for what comes next. If you ask lawyers, they probably misperceive what it is that their role is, Coase would say. He says they'll believe they're deciding whether trees will stand or houses will be in the sun; but Coase says if you think like an economist that probably isn't quite true: The lawyers haven't ended the drama; they've merely opened the curtains for Pareto to enter the stage. Now that they both know who is entitled to what, the question is: Can both of them be made better off by having the winner trade away the right that the court just clarified for them. Suppose this is the case: The neighbor says, "I would gladly trim those trees for $2000"; and the homeowner thinks to himself, "I would gladly pay up to $5000 for an unobstructed sightline to the sun." Any negotiated contract that pays between $2000 and $5000 to have the neighbor voluntarily trim the trees is really going to make both of them better off. The owner of the trees does not have to trim them, but he can if he wants to; the owner of the home can't force the neighbor to trim the trees, but he can pay him to do so; and in this case, a negotiated settlement becomes an efficient outcome. What was the obstacle to this happening before? The obstacle was that there was a lack of clarity as to the rights, so neither party knew what they could negotiate, how they could negotiate. Once that obstacle was overcome, efficiency could prevail; and when efficiency prevails, economists are happier.

How about a little pop quiz at this point? Think like an economist about the contract that those two parties are going to enter into. The wording is going to be very important; why? Because the contract isn't just determining the outcome at this point, the contract is going to define incentives for the future as well; and if it's not carefully worded, you might create a way for your neighbor to generate a very steady stream of income by just keeping on planting more and more fast-growing trees on his property so you have to just keep paying him to keep cutting them down. Thinking about the future consequences of incentives is important as well.

Economists look for these connections between rights and rules and efficiency everywhere; in fact, we've even devoted a subfield in economics to the topic: It goes by the name of law and economics. In that field, the practitioners ask: What are the efficiency consequences of legal rules? They happily find that a lot of rules established by common law precedent with judges and by legislatures really have created incentives that have the result of creating efficient outcomes. Let's take one example, contract law. Contracts are based on voluntary mutual exchanges—and, of course, that's the very foundation definition of efficiency—and the contract law defines which practices are enforceable; defines the consequences of breaking those laws; and, though technically it's resolving past conflicts, most importantly what it's doing is establishing incentives and guidelines for future behavior. Law and economics looks for efficiency in those incentives that arise from the law.

Let's take a couple of examples: First one, the law is only going to enforce bargains that are voluntarily agreed to by all parties. Every signer to a contract must voluntarily and willingly participate; they have to accept all the terms. That fits closely with the presumption of rationality: that the parties who enter a contract must expect their participation to make them better off. Pareto optimality has been the standard in contract law since before Pareto himself was born. Another example: Once the contract has been made, both parties really expect the promises to be kept. That's consistent to what my mom taught me; she said, "A promise is a promise. You keep your word." The law agrees with that most of the time; but occasionally there are rules involving breach where the law actually encourages broken promises. That might be morally wrong, but sometimes it's economically efficient. Let's take a hypothetical; this could be fun.

Let's go back out into the Gulf of Alaska, we'll get on a crab fishing boat; and just before leaving port, the captain is going to meet with the owner of the largest cannery. The cannery has a large order that has to be fulfilled in 10 days; so the cannery owner makes an offer to the captain: "If you will return to port three days before my order is due, I guarantee to pay you $2 a pound for your entire catch." Both parties are better off: The captain of the ship has fixed price and a ready market; the cannery knows there will be a boat there in time to meet its order. But now it gets interesting: The day before our boat is supposed to return, a number of others come into port with a very high catch. The sudden increase in supply causes the price to fall—let's say to $1.80—and the cannery decides to jump in and take advantage; that's less than the $2 it had promised. The cannery is clearly better off, it has a lower price; the captain from whom it buys is better off; but our captain, a party to that original contract, is going to be surprised, he's going to be disappointed, and he's probably going to be pretty angry when he makes port tomorrow to find out that the cannery has breached on the contract, has reneged on its promise.

My mother's rule would have compelled the cannery to wait, fulfill its promise; but the law's more pragmatic, because doing that would have left some money on the table. Our captain was harmed by the breach, no question about it; but he could be made whole, he could achieve the expectation he had, by having the cannery pay damages. What's the standard of damages?

The captain is entitled to the gain he expected when he signed the contract, when he made the bargain; nothing less than that, but also nothing more. If the spot price had risen to $1.90 when our captain pulled into port, the breach by the cannery just cost him $.10 a pound; and when the cannery pays the damages, its net cost also becomes $1.90 a pound, $.10 less than the $2 contract price that it established. With the damages, our captain receives the $2 he expected; the cannery is made better off by the breach because it gets the crab cheaper; our captain is not harmed; the breach is Pareto optimal; each party has an incentive to contract again. Each got at least what they expected.

Let's make this more interesting: Our captain is a man of high emotion. This isn't a business decision for him, this is a personal insult; gentlemen do not do business that way. In order to protest the moral wrong that he has incurred, he anchors just off the dock of the cannery, and he vows to stay until the contract is fulfilled, until they buy his crab for the full $2 a pound. The cannery doesn't need the crab anymore, its order has been fulfilled; and so while he's anchored there, the crabs die. They lose all market value, but our captain has stood his moral ground; and the horrid smell emanating from his hold is testament to his insistence that promises must be kept. He stands awaiting the promised payment, the fulfillment of the contract. He was probably morally right, the cannery was maybe morally wrong; but when the captain goes to court demanding that he be made whole, that the cannery perform and that they buy his crab at $2 a pound—what he expected when he signed the contract—he's going to be very disappointed, because for centuries, judges have imposed a duty on the non-breaching party to mitigate damages. It's childish; worse, it's inefficient to make things worse just out of spite. Those crabs still had value when he reached port; someone would have paid him much more than zero, though perhaps less than $2 a pound. The captain created most of the real damage by willfully destroying his own catch. He should not be rewarded for that, and under law his compensation is going to be limited to the harm that was caused by the cannery: the difference between the contract price and the spot price at the time of breach. Judges probably won't admit it, they often speak in language of justice and fairness, but when you look carefully at it, the evidence is really clear: They seem to know implicitly that when they're resolving past conflicts, they're really defining incentives; and by doing that, they're determining future behavior. More often than not, they've made economic efficiency a foundation for the law.

So where are we now? Today, we've been using this tool kit of ours to examine the way in which rules and rights can be used to shape the incentives and determine the optimal choices of the participants. In some cases, as with the fisheries, getting the incentives right required some kind of external government redefinition of rights. In other situations, as with the ownership of the mechanics' tools, the rights and the rules just seem to have evolved as an ongoing game has played out over time. We've seen how well-defined rights, as with the shade trees and the solar collectors, can open the way to negotiated settlements that will make all the parties involved better off. We've even seen how the law, resolving disputes about the past, is really more importantly defining incentives that are going to guide future decisions and future behavior.

What does all this mean for you? It means that if you're going to think like an economist, you need to ask yourself: Am I in a situation where the rules and the rights are creating some kind of a prisoner's dilemma, establishing incentives that are going to cause each of the participants to make rational decisions that are ultimately going to harm us all? That's what decades-old fishing regulations were doing. We're going to ask: Can the rules or the rights that we have be designed or negotiated to induce individuals to reach better decisions, whether we're talking about creating individual quotas for the fishers; about having mechanics own their own tools; or about having college students share in the benefits of textbook cost reduction? Rights and rules do define incentives; when we set rights and rules now, we're also determining future decisions and future behavior. Anticipating how is a large part of what it means to think like an economist.

Next time, what we're going to do is we're going to begin to consider what happens when some of the incentives that are guiding our choices are really lies in the sense that the prices we pay don't accurately reflect all of the costs inflict or the costs we incur. It's pretty easy to make mistakes in decisions when we have incomplete or distorted information about the consequences of our actions. It's sometimes hard to know what to do when we face inescapable risks. What we're going to be able to do is use these tools we've developed; in the next few lectures, we'll use them to address these challenging questions as well. The next time, we'll begin to do precisely that.

False Incentives, Real Harm
Lecture 5

When you're asked or faced with any issue, to think like an economist is to think: Are there real consequences to a choice that are somehow not being paid for, that are not accounted for, in the incentives facing this decider? How are the false incentives distorting the outcome? Are there mechanisms we can employ to be sure that the consequences are going to be effectively priced? Are there free rider problems here that are preventing our cooperation that would make many of us better off?

Would rational people ever destroy their own planet? Economic thinking teaches us that even though nobody's really in control, individual rational decisions can lead to socially efficient outcomes. But what if people are not considering all of the consequences that their actions have on others? Or what if the incentives that people are given are simply inaccurate? One kind of inaccuracy that is important to economists is externalities, which occur any time we take an action that creates a benefit for somebody else or imposes a cost on somebody else with no payment made. When externalities exist, rational individual decisions can lead to inefficient outcomes in 2 distinct ways: False incentives may cause us to make decisions that cause significant harm to other people, or we may fail to consider choices that would cause benefit.

The dilemma of global warming is an example of the tragedy of the commons. A commons is something that we all use collectively and no one is directly responsible for. The presumption is that we'll all use the commons responsibly, but the incentives for each user of a commons work against that hope. If other people pay the costs, I get protected without doing a thing; I can be what economists call a free rider. There are 2 practical ways to try to overcome the free rider problem: compulsory participation (e.g., taxation) and linking the public good to a desirable private good (e.g., getting people to pay voluntarily).

There are strong economic forces incentivizing us to use the atmosphere as a free-for-all dump for greenhouse gases. Any solution to this problem will be a public good of mammoth proportions: There are 6 billion people, all of whom have an incentive to try to ride for free. Thinking like an economist helps define how much our behavior ought to change and gives us some guidance on what kind of policies we could use to make that happen. How much of a reduction in greenhouse gases makes sense? If you want to answer a question about optimality, you go to the margin. Some carbon dioxide in the atmosphere is natural; the question is how much of it would be optimal. When the gain from reducing a unit of emission has fallen down to meet the rising cost of reducing it, we've hit the equimarginal principle. Once we've identified the desired level, how do we get there? To an economist, the answer's simple: The problem is caused by the fact that the price is wrong, so change the price. If we were to put a price on pollution—say, $100 per ton—then every time you emit a ton, you have to pay a real cost. If you can reduce your emissions at a cost of less than $100 a ton, economic logic alone says do it. You don't need a mandate; the invisible hand will take care

Global warming is an example of the tragedy of the commons.

of everything. Economists started making this argument back in the 1960s, and people thought it was a crazy idea. But now, putting a price on pollution is embraced by policy makers all over the world as the most plausible hope for impacting global climate change. An additional practical advantage to pricing pollution, rather than just regulating and restricting, is that when we need to change the pollution target, we just adjust the price—players will adjust their behavior at the margin.

Unfortunately, it's not as simple as just applying what economists know to solve the problem; policy makers have to actually make it happen. The invisible hand can lead to conflict and paralysis in the political arena. Politicians, like the rest of us, respond to incentives. Each actor prefers a solution to climate change that's paid for by somebody else; the benefits from being a free rider on the global scale are huge. Politicians in each nation know they will be punished back home if they take a large share of the costs. But without enough paying passengers, this train is not going to leave the station. That outcome would be both individually rational and collectively tragic. ■

Take-Away Points

1. When the incentives facing decision makers do not accurately reflect the true costs and benefits of their actions (i.e., externalities), rational individual decisions can result in damaging and inefficient outcomes.

2. Individual incentives to be a free rider can prevent voluntary solutions to public goods problems, such as brush fire prevention or greenhouse gas reduction. Overcoming free riding requires either compulsory contributions or a linked connection with an excludable private good.

False Incentives, Real Harm
Lecture 5—Transcript

We're back again for the fifth in our lecture series on "How to Think Like an Economist." We have a toolkit, six Foundation Principles, we have three Core Concepts, and we've developed this central conclusion that even though nobody's really in control, individual rational decisions can lead to socially efficient outcomes. But the big question: Are they always going to do that? Behind that central conclusion, there are a whole lot of "ifs," "ands," or "buts"; and the last time we talked about the importance of having well-defined rights and rules if we're going to have effective and efficient outcomes. But today I want to turn to another "if," this time a really big "if," an "if" that's so big and so broad that it's going to lead us to one of the fundamental questions of the modern era; and that is simply this: Would rational people ever destroy their own planet?

What if the incentives that people are using to guide these choices are lies; what if they don't tell the truth about costs and benefits; what if they're not considering all of the consequences that our actions have on others; or what if the incentives are simply inaccurate? There's one kind of inaccuracy that economists spend a lot of time talking about, and that's called an "externality." Any time I take an action that creates a benefit for somebody else or imposes a cost on somebody else, but no payment has to be made, I don't have to be paid for it; I don't have to pay them for the cost. When externalities exist, then rational individual decisions can lead to inefficient outcomes in two distinct ways: The first one is that the false incentives may cause us to make decisions that are really causing significant, real harm to other people; that's avoidable, but we don't consider it. The other is that sometimes externalities will prevent us from making decisions, making choices, that are really going to cause benefit, but we don't consider that.

I think I'm going to tell you about this, we can see both of these at play, in what I'm going to call, for want of a better word, "A Tale of Two Fires." Here we are: You're the dispatcher for the emergency services in Cleveland, Ohio, and you get a call. "The Cuyahoga River's on fire." Of course, you're a little bit puzzled by this; you want to know more details: "Do you mean the brush along the river is on fire? Do you mean some of the buildings along the river are on fire?" But the improbable truth is the river itself was on fire. Some smoker walking across a bridge took a last puff and flicked it into the river; instead of going out, the river went "whoosh" and caught fire. The truth is that so many factories had been using that river as a dump for volatile chemicals that the liquid that was flowing north toward Lake Erie couldn't really be called "water" at all, and the flames that were leaping from the surface gave certain proof of that.

I honestly don't know how they ultimately extinguished that fire; they certainly didn't just get the pumps out and spray more river water onto it. But the flammability of that river, and the subsequent fire, were the unfortunate results of behavior; behavior that was probably irresponsible, I know it was harmful, but it wasn't in the economists' strict sense irrational. I want to think economically for a moment or two about the kind of incentives that the polluters of that river faced; and the fire, like some other disasters, was ultimately inevitable, given the incentives that they all faced. The invisible hand was at work, and it was giving that river a pretty bad beating.

It's an example of what Garrett Hardin, in his classic 1968 article in the journal *Science*, called the "Tragedy of the Commons." A "commons" is something that we all get to use collectively, and no one is directly responsible for. Boston Common was a pasture that everyone shared. The air, oceans, outer space, and rivers are really owned by no one, and thus they're available to all of us without any real cost. The presumption is that we'll all use the commons responsibly; but the incentives for each user of a commons—a commons like the Cuyahoga River—really work against that hope, because this is the Prisoner's Dilemma all over again. Each potential polluter, each person along the side of that river, had two options: The first option was to incur substantial costs to capture, treat, and carefully dispose of all its chemical waste; and the second option was pay nothing and dump it in the river. The first option had high costs; for the polluter, the second one had none.

Even if believe it's wrong to dump into the river, I probably had little choice. Here's why: If my competitors on the river are dumping and I don't, I'm at a significant cost disadvantage. I go broke; my competitors thrive; the river's polluted anyway; and in short, harsh terms, if others pollute, the game theory incentives are "I should either pollute also or I'm going to go broke." What if everyone else stops polluting? If I continue, I'm going to be at a major cost advantage. My competitors will suffer; I'll thrive; the river will be much cleaner; and they will have paid all the cost. In short, harsh terms: If others don't do the polluting, I'll do better by polluting. What's the payoff matrix? If they pollute, my best strategy is to continue polluting. If they don't pollute, my best strategy is to continue polluting. No matter what course others may take, "pollute" is the best individual strategy. Rational individuals all made decisions that led them to be collectively worse off; they did what the incentives said they should do, but they and the river all "got burned."

But there's something extra here; there's something different about this. Remember our original version of the Prisoner's Dilemma, and people engaged in selfish, strategic behavior that ended up harming them both? Here it's different, because much of the cost from that fire was borne by innocent bystanders, by people whose lives are negatively affected by all of this: they're exposed to toxic chemicals, they live near a burning river. They didn't participate in the decisions; they didn't decide to pollute; but they're feeling the weight of the consequences. Apparently Adam Smith's invisible hand can push bystanders over a cliff. The response to the individual incentives assured harm rather than social gain.

What, to an economist, had gone so horribly wrong? Moral failings? Undoubtedly. Callous irresponsibility? Certainly. But more than that, the incentives that the polluters faced were wrong; they didn't reflect the costs of the actions actually being taken. There were costs external to the decision makers, but they had no need to consider those. Remember the foundation principle we had, principle number two? There's no such thing as a free lunch. There's no such thing as a free river, either. When they used that river as a chemical dump, they were giving up the opportunity for it to be used for other valued purposes: It could not be home for fish; it could not be used as a swimming hole on a hot summer day; it could not be drinking water for a city in need; that as long as we're living near a city like that, a number of opportunities for healthful living and long life were forever gone. There was a price to be paid for using that as a chemical dump, but the price wasn't paid by the people making the decision; the price that the polluters had to pay was a lie. Garret Hardin's choice of terms in his decision was apt: The outcome in Cleveland was truly tragic, and it was the result of false incentives.

The second fire: Let's travel 22 years later, we'll go 2,000 miles away. On a single afternoon, there was a fire raging in the Oakland Hills above the San Francisco Bay. For years, drought had accumulated a tremendous amount of tinder-dry brush on the hillsides, and thousands of homes perched on the pinnacles were in great peril. They awaited simply a single spark and a windy day. They would have been much better off if there was some way to get that danger away; but there it was, year after year, adding fuel, making it more and more dangerous. Everyone who lived in that community would have been better off if that brush had been removed, but it was in no one's—no one person's—interest to go to the effort to remove it; because that fire protection is what economists tend to call a "public" good or a "non-excludable" good. Fire prevention? Fire prevention is something that either everyone has it or no one has it; it's an all or nothing proposition. There's no way that we can protect every other house on a street from a raging fire; it's either we protect all, or we protect none.

Here's the other side of this: If other people will pay the costs, go to the effort to clear the brush, I get protected and I don't have to do a thing; I can be what economists call a "free rider," I'll go along without picking up the tab. But if lots of other people don't decide to engage in protection, then that danger is going to be there no matter how much I clear the brush around my house; the fire will spread, there's no reason for me to incur those costs alone.

There's an economist by the name of Mancur Olson, and he wrote an interesting book talking about the intractability of this free rider problem. He says that this is going to increase and become more difficult as the size of the group gets bigger and bigger. I think I mentioned last time Robert Frost's famous poem about the neighbors who meet once a year to repair the rock wall (I bring it up because I don't really know that many poems, so I have to come back to the same one twice). But what they were doing is the two of them were joining and putting a boundary between their properties; and it was pretty obvious with just two people, if one of them hadn't showed up, if one had tried to ride free, the endeavor to fix the wall—and likely the wall itself—would have collapsed. If you don't have the participation of both, then the benefit would have been available to neither one.

But that was a group of two, and free riding is hard to pull off in a group that small. But in the Oakland Hills above the San Francisco Bay on that October afternoon, there were thousands and thousands of people, all of whom were going to be affected by the ability to eliminate the fire danger. Voluntary cooperation is exponentially harder to attain when every person is so small relative to it that neither his participation nor his nonparticipation is going to have any impact at all on the outcome. There are two results: The first is I have an incentive to free ride; and the second is I know that other people have an incentive to free ride as well, and I certainly don't want to be the one standing here paying their fare. The result is none of us are really prevented from facing that fire danger, because we could not get together in order to clean it up. Everyone in the Oakland Hills was aware of this danger, but it was no one's job to clear the brush; it was no one's job to organize others to do so. On that one October afternoon, 3,000 homes on the top of those hills all went up in smoke. Reliance on several thousand people to all have to get together and agree to provide that public good didn't work out here. There were simply too many people, each of whom was too small compared to the result, to have individually rational decisions lead to acceptably good outcomes.

With public goods, there are two practical ways that we've come up with to try and overcome this free rider problem. The first one's fairly obvious: compulsory participation. Governments will make you pay through tax-funded programs, or sometimes an organization, a neighborhood, will have a mandatory neighborhood association fee. But there's another way that some groups use: If you can link the public good to a desirable private good, you can get people to participate. Here's an example: I promise you that AARP (the American Association of Retired Persons) could never support its very extensive political lobbying effort—which is a clear public good; you can ride for free on it without participating—simply from voluntary contributions; "Give us money, and we'll lobby for interests for the elderly." It succeeds by linking its memberships to private individual benefits. If you want the health insurance, you want the travel discounts, you want the other private benefits of AARP, you must become a member; and that provides them with the funds for their political activities.

Now let's broaden our horizons even a little bit more. Let's talk about the Tragedy of the Commons on a global scale. The problem that we face of individuals trying to optimize but facing false incentives leads to social tragedies not just in burning rivers and burnt out neighborhoods; U.N. scientists have told us we face this on a grander scale in the entire globe. "Climate change," they report, "is a threat to humanity as a whole." You don't have to be an economist to think that the extinction of the human species is probably an undesirable, and even inefficient, outcome. Of course, there's still a good deal of debate about how much human responsibility there is for global climate change, and I won't try to resolve the science for you today. But economics, with its emphasis on incentives, says that there really are strong forces for all of us to use this earth atmosphere as a free-for-all dump for greenhouse gases. It's the Cuyahoga River all over again, but this time writ large. This is the problem, the tragedy, of the commons on a truly global scale.

Any solution to this is going to have to be a public good of mammoth proportions: six billion people, all of whom have an incentive to try to ride for free. Yet here we are; we're "lifers" in this global prison. That makes any possible disaster from climate change a problem I think we should think about; and I think we can think about it as economists to. Let's try that. If the problem is that the incentives people are using to make decisions are false, what does economic thinking tell us about making them true? The first thing thinking like an economist does: It helps defines how much our behavior ought to change, what's the optimal amount of change; and second, it gives us some guidance on what kind of policies we could use to make it happen.

Let's consider each of these in turn. The first question is: How much of a reduction in greenhouse gases makes sense? You know where an economist is going to go on this one: If you want to answer a question about optimality, you go to the margin. Of course, we think that the marginal value or the marginal cost of having one more or one less always depends on how much of it you already have. Some rain is beneficial; too much can be catastrophic (just ask Noah). Similarly, some CO_2 in the atmosphere is natural, it's something that we expect; nature requires it. Policy and practical choice is not "Shall there be CO_2 or shall there be no CO_2"; the question is always with economists, "How much of it would be optimal?"

Think like an economist for a moment about that principle. Remember we talked about the optimal level of emissions, and that's going to depend on the costs and benefits on the margin. We could get rid of climate change by exterminating all human activity, but I don't think that's a very good idea; or we could completely ignore climate change and risk exterminating all human life, but I don't think that's a particularly good idea either; so we're looking for something in the middle, an optimal level of emissions that should be our target. Of course, for an economist, that means balancing the marginal cost of CO_2 with the marginal cost of reducing. As emissions are reduced, the harm done by the last ton—the amount of the marginal harm done—is getting smaller; so as we have less and less emissions, the marginal cost is going down. But as we push our technology and try and get rid of more and more emissions, the marginal cost of getting rid of that last, that next, ton of CO_2 emissions is going up.

We're back at Econ 101: When the gain from reducing another emission has fallen down to meet the rising cost of doing it, just stop. Where are we? We've hit the equimarginal principle my friends; we've satisfied that. The solution is efficient; we have optimized. I'm going to have to leave it to scientists to figure out what the actual measures are of cost, particularly those with environmental terms; but economic thinking helps us understand that standard of finding this balance.

Once that's been done, there's a second question; and this is one where economists have perhaps more value to offer: How do you go about getting to that level? Of course, the answer's simple: If the problem is caused by the fact that the price is wrong, change the price. Let's see how: If we were to put a price on pollution—we set a price, say, $100 per ton—then every time you emit a ton, you have to pay a real cast cost; it would be part of your calculations; you'd have to consider those emissions every time you did something in the business world. If you can reduce your emissions at a cost of less than $100 a ton, economic logic alone says do it; you don't need detailed regulation, you just need your accountants to show you the money going in versus the money being saved. If we can develop new technologies so that we could reduce emissions, economic logic says we'll do that; you'll save money by doing it. You don't need a mandate, it's the invisible hand; its direct benefits that come from reducing emissions, as long as the cost is below the price. The individual hand is going to be enough punishment for those who don't look for cost effective ways to reduce emissions.

This sounds morally wrong; it says that people, in effect, can pay and continue emitting greenhouse gases. But remember the goal of this whole thing? It's a good result. We want sustainable global levels of greenhouse emissions, a good result; not good behavior, per se. Economists' logic, that's the way they think about these things: that if price is going to be the cheapest way to reduce emissions, all we have to do is put a price on emitting. Economists started making this argument I think back in the 1960s, and when they first espoused it, everybody said, "That's a crazy idea; economists have the nuttiest point of view in the world." But now, 40–50 years later, that whole idea of putting a price on pollution is being embraced by policymakers all over the world. It seems to be the most plausible and most effective hope for any real impact on global climate change. Who would have imagined that?

There are additional practical advantages to pricing pollution, rather than just regulating and restricting. For example, if we get new evidence that says the target is too high (or too low), we don't have to rewrite volumes of regulations; we don't have to put in different metering equipment. All you do is adjust the price, and then individuals are going to make their own adjustments of their behavior at the margin.

Let's talk more about how we go about doing this. Economists agree almost to a person that some price for emissions is the most efficient and effective solution when and if governments decide that something must be done. Economists don't agree on a lot, but they do agree that a price is the best solution for this externality problem. They differ somewhat on what kind of a price: There's some who would like a direct, wide-based carbon tax where every user of energy—households, transportation, industry—all pay a carbon tax. But others kind of like that fisheries solution we talked about last time; the idea of putting a total limit on and allowing people to trade within that. They call that a "cap and trade" system, and the idea would be that scientists somehow would agree on a total global cap, the total amount of emissions that the environment can really sustain, and then it would issue permits to emitters, allowing them to emit up to some amount as long as the total of the permits was less than the total cap. That's the "cap" part of "cap and trade."

But economists like the other part, too, the part that says "trade." If there isn't any trade, then for permit holders, the price of polluting is zero up to the permit, but it's infinite for others; they can emit nothing at all. No matter how easy it would be for a permit holder to reduce emissions, they have no incentive to do that; non-holders would have to shut down. You do reach the cap limit, but there's no price to respond to; and that seems both inefficient and unfair. But if the holders of the permits were able to sell their permits, then if they had a way to reduce emissions inexpensively they could make money by reducing their emissions and selling the permit to someone else. It would be a better off solution for both the seller and the buyer. If non-users find that they cannot reduce emissions very well, they could buy that from someone else; and what this price does is it makes you recognize the opportunity cost. Emitting CO_2 has a cost in the market, and not taking advantage of reductions is leaving—something economists don't like—money on the table.

The reductions in this case are always made by the emitters who can do it most cheaply; and who figures out who can do that most cheaply? The individual players do; and the market moves those permits to where they can do the most good. All the trades are mutually beneficial and socially beneficial. The global reduction in emissions is done at the lowest possible total social cost; Pareto is happy; economists are satisfied. That's the good news: The true price for using for the atmosphere could save the planet from devastating climate change. Unfortunately, there's some bad news as well, because now that we economists know what ought to happen, policymakers are going to have to be the ones who actually make it happen; they're going to have to reach some consensus on the details of how to go about doing this. As policymakers often say, the devil is in the details.

Let's think like economists for a moment about the processes of making collective policy decisions as opposed to those individual rational decisions that we've talked about before. When we think about policy making, implementing either of those solutions on a worldwide basis is going to be very, very difficult. Remember economists? We think, in our fundamental principles, that people behave strategically; not just when we're shopping, but when we're making policy as well. When we begin to talk about charging people to use something like the environment that's always before been absolutely free of charge—not costless, mind you, but free of charge—we're unquestionably now in the world of politics. Believe me, policy making is not a process of voluntary Pareto trades; it has winners, it has losers. Rational people pretty much always want to be in the winner's circle; very seldom do they prefer to be in the loser's circle. The invisible hand—that persistent drive to respond to incentives that can make people work together, that can make us cooperate in mutual exchanges where both of us win—can lead to conflict and paralysis in the political arena where gains and losses are distributed and redistributed.

Over 50 years ago, an economist named Anthony Downs wrote a classic book called *An Economic Theory of Democracy*. He took our basic toolkit, and he used it to look at electoral politics and policymaking. He stared with a simple premise: Politicians, like all the rest of us, respond to incentives; and if they want to continue being politicians, they're going to have to adopt their policy positions to maximize their votes. In essence, it's this: If, like Henry Clay, they'd rather be right rather than President, they almost always get their wish. If they truly want to be President, or Senator, or Representative, or even Mayor, they'd better be ready to do what's politic. I know that's cynical, but it's the logical application of economic thinking to political behavior. In our next lecture, we're going to see how this can lead to some very troubling conclusions about electoral processes.

But for now, consider for a moment just trying to implement either one of these policies regarding climate change. Any time we're going to put a price on emissions or establish a system of tradable permits, that's a new set of direct, cash on the barrel head, out of my pocket costs, paid by people who up until now haven't had to pay a cent to use the atmosphere; and each of those people—or probably I should say each of us people—also knows that their own behavior is so insignificant in terms of the global outcome that what I do won't really have an impact on global warming. Each of us is going to be better off if we can ride for free; if we can somehow get somebody else to pay the cost of reduced emissions. If I can get on that "save the Earth" train without a ticket, then each of us is likely to turn to the political system and see if they can do that, without having to buy the ticket. Even if I am individually willing to pay my fair share, I don't know that I want to be the one to pay for everybody else's free ride; I want a system where they're picking up as much of the tab as possible.

In principle, we can all agree that a price would have to be paid to stop climate change, but we also can disagree about who should pay that price. Who's going to get those emission permits; are they going to be issued free of charge to current emitters? Isn't that some way to reward peoples' past behavior? Maybe we should auction them off; but if we do that, aren't family firms, smaller firms, going to be priced out of the market? Aren't their vote-conscious representatives going to stand in Congress and say, "We cannot adopt the policy that punishes the small American businessperson?" Each of us prefers a pricing solution for this that's paid by somebody else's constituents. Remember how hard it was for the residents of Oakland to save their neighborhood by cooperating and getting rid of all that built up fuel that was accumulating on the slopes? If they'd done so, they might have saved their homes; but it just didn't happen.

Compare that to trying to address global warming and that problem seems like a trivial event indeed. The benefits from being a free rider in that scale are much too great; it's true for individuals, and it's true for nations. If the U.S. can get China or Brazil or Europe to restrict their emissions, then we don't have to so much, because it's the same atmosphere, it's the same commons. India, China, and other developing nations argue—perhaps with validity—that the West, industrialized for two centuries, helped this buildup of greenhouse gases, and now it seems unfair to ask India and China to slow their growth and freeze the relative wealth after the damage has been done. They argue that the West caused the harm, the East shouldn't be asked to bear the burden of fixing it.

If Downs is correct—and I think he is—then the obstacles to a solution here are pretty great. The politicians in each nation have no choice but to respond to the interests back home. They know they're going to be punished if they take a large share of the costs; they know they'll be rewarded if we can make the rest of the world ride free. But without enough paying passengers, this train is not going to leave the station; and that outcome would be both individually rational and collectively tragic.

What are we going to take away from all this? First, of course, understanding how economists think about really crucial policy problems like global climate change is part of being a good citizen; it's something I think everyone should know. But on a smaller scale, when you're asked or faced with any issue, to think like an economist is to think: Are there real consequences to a choice that are somehow not being paid for, that are not accounted for, in the incentives facing this decider? How are the false incentives distorting the outcome? Are there mechanisms we can employ to be sure that the consequences are going to be effectively priced? Are there free rider problems here that are preventing our cooperation that would make many of us better off? Could we overcome them doing something like the AARP does?

In the next three lectures, we'll think in some more detail about the economics particularly of information; because how can we make intelligent choices if we don't have good information? We'll see how that relates to rational decision making and to the consequences of doing that.

The Economics of Ignorance
Lecture 6

When computers first came out, there was a principle that was adopted that still holds called the GIGO principle: garbage in, you're going to get garbage out. I think there's kind of a GIGO to life as well: If you get garbage info in before you make your decision process, the decisions you make are likely to be garbage as well.

Rational decision making is dependent more than anything else on the quality of the information that you have. Suboptimal information will likely lead to poor decisions. Economically speaking, for each decision there's an optimal level of ignorance—you need to examine the trade-offs between ignorance and information.

How much information, and how much ignorance, is optimal? Is it the same for every decision? As always, we look at the marginal benefit and the marginal cost of information. What does more information buy you? If you have more information, there's a reduced chance that you'll make a suboptimal decision. Sometimes the difference between choices is trivial: The movie I chose to see was awful; I would have enjoyed the other one more. Sometimes the difference is monumental: If I had gone to the doctor before my disease became terminal, my life would have been saved. The size benefit from making the right choice, or the cost of making the wrong choice, is what establishes one of the parameters—the maximum possible value of information. It would have been irrational for me to spend $100 buying information about movie choices before I went to the theater. But I should have paid far more than that to go see the doctor.

No matter what that maximum is, at some point the marginal value of information starts to decline. When I know a lot, a little more information doesn't add that much. Also, when I'm acquiring information, some of it's easy to acquire, but at some point the marginal cost of getting more starts to rise. When the marginal value of information and the marginal cost of acquiring information are equal to each other, the equimarginal principle has been satisfied. We have defined the optimal amount of information, as well as the optimal level of ignorance—to acquire information beyond that point would be irrational.

How can individuals overcome some of the costs of ignorance and decrease our vulnerability to bad decisions? Is there a way to aggregate and use the collective knowledge out there in the world? One finding from experiments and studies is that if we take many independent estimates and average them, they can yield information better than any one participant can generate. That is much of what's behind economists' affinity for markets. Markets provide an inexpensive, accurate, and valuable way to take a lot of information and compress it into a clear and accessible form.

Prices can give us a lot of important information about the wisdom of the crowd, but sometimes we need information that price alone isn't enough to carry. Depending on incentives, this information may be gathered by individuals, private entities, or governments. Another way we acquire information at lower costs is in the principal-agent relationship. We pay somebody more knowledgeable than ourselves to make important decisions for us. An obvious case of this is diagnostic physicians: When we are having chest pains and shortness of breath, it's too late to start applying to medical school. Instead, we turn to experts who provide us with this knowledge.

People must balance the cost of acquiring more information with the cost of making wrong decisions.

Where does this leave us? Complete ignorance is certainly not bliss: It leads to bad decisions, often with harsh consequences. On the other hand, complete omniscience is neither humanly possible nor affordable.

When the marginal value of information and the marginal cost of acquiring information are equal to each other, the equimarginal principle has been satisfied.

The human dilemma is to navigate rationally between these 2 extremes, balancing the costs of making wrong decisions with the costs of acquiring more information. How do you apply this in your daily life? You should base the amount of investment you make for information on the size of the cost if you make a wrong decision. When information is widely scattered, you can look for processes, like markets, that aggregate and compress the information to see if it reveals the wisdom of a crowd. But remember to ask yourself the following: Is this a situation where there are multiple people making truly independent evaluations, or is this a structure where each is just repeating what others have said? Finally, you should turn to expert advice to reduce the cost of overcoming ignorance, but only if it is in the expert's best interest to disseminate unbiased information. As always, economic thinking involves a consideration of incentives—yours and everyone else's. ∎

The Economics of Car Safety Information

One thing we all care about is the crashworthiness of our cars. We could try to buy one of each model of car and crash it into a wall, but that would be prohibitively expensive. This is valuable information for me, but I can't produce it myself. Are there incentives for someone else to do that for me?

That's a complicated question. Information used by one can be equally valuable to other people, and information isn't like an ice cream cone—if one person consumes it, it's not gone; it's still available to others. This is good because there's the potential for us to divide up the extraordinary cost, produce the information once, and then share it and use it many times. The shared cost for each of us will be less than the combined benefit will be. The unfortunate part is that collecting that information is similar to cleaning up the atmosphere: Everybody wants to do it, but nobody really wants to pay for it. If I can wait and get enough others to chip in and pay for the crash test results, I get them for nothing. Voluntary cooperation among 250 million Americans is not likely to occur. Could an entrepreneur come along and make a profit by conducting these tests and selling the results? Maybe, but there are obstacles: Once the first few sales are made, the information is impossible to control and the profit potential disappears.

Yet information on crashworthiness does get generated; it's made available to the public free of charge. Who has an incentive to do that? Actually, there are 2 sets of crash test data that get generated. The first is produced by the National Highway Traffic Safety Administration, which solves the free rider problem by drawing its funding from our compulsory taxes. There's a second group, the Insurance Institute for Highway Safety, that is benefited by getting that expensive information and giving it away for free. Insurance companies' profits decrease when people drive less crashworthy cars, so the more information in consumers' hands, the higher the insurance companies' profits. How do you get the widest distribution possible on information? You make it free.

Take-Away Points

1. Because information is costly, for each decision there is a rational degree of ignorance, beyond which the marginal cost of additional information would be greater than its marginal cost.

2. It is rational (and wise) to seek or devise mechanisms or relationships to reduce the cost of acquiring information. Examples include artificial markets such as the Iowa Electronic Markets (to realize the potential wisdom of the crowd) and principal-agent relationships (to capitalize on the resaleability of expertise).

The Economics of Ignorance
Lecture 6—Transcript

Welcome back for one more time. Today we're going to use Lecture 6 in our series on "How to Think Like an Economist." Much of our time has been spent trying to figure out how to make rational decisions; but rational decision making is probably dependent more than anything else on the quality of the information that you have. When computers first came out, there was a principle that was adopted that still holds called the "GIGO Principle": garbage in, you're going to get garbage out. I think there's kind of a GIGO to life as well: If you get garbage info in before you make your decision process, the decisions you make are likely to be garbage as well. It's so important, in fact, that for the next three lectures we're going to spend a lot of time talking about different aspects of thinking like economists about information.

"If you think education is expensive you should try ignorance." That's a bumper sticker I often see on cars driving around my over-educated college town; and I know you're saying, "Here he goes again, what kind of a professor uses bumper stickers as illustration points?" But I do it a lot. I understand what that sentiment is, I understand what they mean to say; but if you think about it like an economist, you know it mischaracterizes the choice we have to make. Why? The choice is never between omniscience on the one hand and total ignorance on the other; this is a choice about tradeoffs on the margin. As always, there's an optimal balance between the costs of acquiring information and the costs of being ignorant; and as much as it pains me as a college professor to admit it, there is such a thing as having too much education. In this lecture and the two that follow, we're going to address a number of variations on that theme; we're going to examine some tradeoffs between ignorance and information. Economically speaking, for each decision there's going to be an optimal level of ignorance. We'll use our toolkit to explore that—the same six Foundation Principles, the same Core Concepts, and that Pareto standard of economic efficiency—and we're going to reach the conclusion that a certain amount of ignorance almost always makes sense.

It's not that information isn't valuable, obviously it is; and it's not that having more and better information doesn't lead to better decisions, because it does. More information is valuable, more information does aid decisions, but you know what I'm going to say next: There's no such thing as a free lunch; there's no such thing as truly free information as well. Information always has a cost; if nothing else, it takes time and effort to absorb it and assimilate it. If you spend two hours down at the library reading free materials that has its own cost; an opportunity cost, perhaps, not a direct financial one. But in order to be rational, the benefit of more information must always be balanced off with its cost.

Economics, as you know, is all about making choices; and it's hard to overemphasize the significance of information. If we don't know what the alternatives are, if we don't know what the consequences of those alternatives are going to be, it's going to be very hard for us to choose wisely between the options that are available to us. Information is essential for optimization. Yet we enter this world not with optimization, but—if you'll allow me to coin a new term—we enter with "omnignorance"; we know virtually nothing. We run high risks of making bad decisions, and the acquisition of information is itself costly. One of the key decisions we make over and over and over again: How ignorant is it rational for me to be?

In this lecture, I want to make an assumption, a metaphor, that we'll say that the essential information is out there somewhere, and our problem is how do we go about getting it and how much should we get? Conceptualize information: a giant pile big pile of data, a giant pile of sand. Nobody owns it, nobody controls it, it's just there; we can go get it when we want. But it's bulky, so we have to make repeated trips; and each time we can get a bit of it or a bundle of it or a bucket of it, and we bring that back and evaluate and, of course, that's our marginal information, what we acquire in each trip. There are real opportunity costs in doing that, and I'm going to assume as I have more and more information here to work with, the value of getting just one more bit at some point starts to decline. We've reached the term "diminishing returns." At some point, getting another bit of information won't really add much, and won't be worth the cost of going after it.

That's too simplified; and later we'll get much more complicated. We'll worry about the world when there are chance events and risk and probability coming in; we'll worry about what happens when other people control that information and can use it strategically to try and influence us. But for today, for today alone, we're going to put those complexities aside and focus on this simpler problem: How much information, and how much ignorance, is optimal? Is it the same for every decision? If not, what determines the amount of information/ignorance in a different decision? Are there things we can do to try and reduce the amount of ignorance to make information more accessible? To an economist, of course, this is all going to depend—and you know where we're going—on the marginal benefit and the marginal cost of information. What does more information buy you? What it does: If you have more information, there's a reduced chance that you're going to make a suboptimal, a not so good, decision; and the cost of making a bad decision is what happens if you make the perfect one relative what happens if you make the less good one. Sometimes that difference is trivial: The movie I chose to see was awful. I would have enjoyed the other one more. Sometimes the difference between choices is monumental: If I had gone to the doctor before my disease became terminal, my life would have been saved.

The size benefit from making the right choice, or alternatively the cost of making the wrong choice, is what establishes one of the parameters, one of the maximum possible values of information. It would have been irrational, perhaps even downright stupid, for me to spend $100 buying information about movie choices before I went to the theater. I'm sure that cost is many times what it would have been worth to know. But I should have paid far more than that to go see the doctor; the size of making that wrong decision is so extraordinary that it would have justified an immense amount of investment and information. The size of the wrong decision defines one of the parameters for the optimal degree of ignorance.

No matter what that maximum is, it's also true that at some point, as I say, the marginal value of information starts to decline. When I know a lot, a little more information doesn't add that much; but similarly, it also means that when I'm acquiring information, some of it's easy to acquire, but at some point as I try to get more and more information the marginal cost of getting more is going to start to rise. When the marginal value of information is coming down, and the marginal cost of acquiring information is rising, there's an optimal point; there's a sticking point there, and you know where it is: where they're equal to each other. The equimarginal principle has been satisfied, and that's the optimal amount of information. It also defines what the optimal level of ignorance is; to acquire information beyond that point would be irrational.

When you think about information and ignorance, it can lead to some fairly depressing kinds of conclusions to contemplate. I don't know if you remember the last lecture, we talked about Anthony Downs's classic book, *An Economic Theory of Democracy*, where he thought like an economist about electoral democracy and the processes in it. One of the questions he asked is: What's the optimal level of ignorance, what's the optimal investment in information, for a rational voter? Of course, when you go into the polling place and you cast your ballot, you care about future policies. But you're not voting for future policies; you're voting for an individual who may or may not face a whole lot of different policy decisions at some time in the future that may or may not have an impact upon you. To know how the future candidate might behave in all those cases would be a huge investment in inventory. We'd have to evaluate all possible policies, we'd have to do it for all possible candidates, and that would be an extraordinary investment. That's the cost; what would be the benefit of being an informed voter? The benefit of being an informed voter would be that you might reduce the probability of making the wrong policy choice versus the right one. Here's where it gets interesting: the difference between a well-cast vote and a poorly-cast vote, multiplied by the probability that your one vote is going to determine the outcome of the election; because if it doesn't, then there's no real benefit to being informed at all. That means that the actual benefit to being an informed voter in pure rationality terms is almost always just about zero.

Downs ends up in his book by saying, "For a great many citizens in a democracy, rational behavior excludes any investment in political information." That's a depressing conclusion; it's one that I'm horrified to see before me. I hesitate but have to tell you: It's empirically verified far more often than not. The National Election Survey gets undertaken each election year, and it finds—listen to this—that only 15 percent of Americans can even name, just name, one candidate for the House of Representatives from their own district; and only 4 percent can name two candidates from their own district. If Americans don't even know the names of the candidates, it seems unlikely that they're going to know a whole lot about their policy positions that may or may not in the future be taken. It may be wrong to be an uninformed voter, but it isn't, sadly, irrational; and even more sadly, it's certainly not uncommon.

In a later lecture, we're going to come back to this and look at political campaigns as a way to process and exploit this rational ignorance. But for now, I want to consider some innovations; some rational ways that we have developed or might develop to try and overcome some of these costs of ignorance, and overcome our own vulnerability to some bad decisions. Remember, right now we're operating with this metaphor that the information we need is out there, it's just too expensive to acquire. There's a lot of it; it's scattered all over the place; many people have information relative to what we need to know; and collectively we know more than any of us knows individually. But, of course, it's the individual that has to make a rational decision; so there's a problem. Is there a way to aggregate and use that collective knowledge? There's a man named James Surowieki who's written just a fascinating little book that he calls *The Wisdom of Crowds*. In that, he looks at a whole number of ways in which processes have been established or experiments have been undertaken to see what we can learn about collecting that information and putting it into a useful form.

He cites some simple and very intriguing examples: Experimenters—and this is something I guess psychologists do—will ask a large number of people independently to guess the number of beans in a jar; so they have a jar and they say, "How many beans are in this?" You know that the guesses are going to be all over the place; some will be way too high, some will be way too low. But the extraordinary thing is that if you take the average of those guesses, it's likely to be very close to the real number. He concludes that if you were to run 10 different jelly-bean-counting experiments, it's likely that each time one or two students would do better than the group, be closer to the real average, but it wouldn't be the same students every time. Over the 10 experiments, the group's performance is almost certainly going to be the best possible. Surowieki finds that interesting, but he uses it to go to far more significant events. I want to tell you a story, and this is one that I find absolutely astounding.

In 1968, an American submarine disappeared somewhere in the North Atlantic, and the Navy had had no success in finding where it was. This young officer—and I don't know where he got the idea—came up with a unique process. He gathered a whole panel of experts, who understood about submarines and understood the geography and the geology of the North Atlantic, and he isolated them; he put them apart from each other. He gave them all the data and asked them to independently estimate what could have been the cause and what would be the location where the submarine had gone down. They couldn't discuss their theories with each other; they couldn't influence one or convince somebody else that their idea was wrong; he wanted independent expert opinions. Then he used something that's called Bayesian analysis, and he found a way to take all these estimates and average them to the group's prediction of the location where the missing sub could be found. Not one of the individual estimates was very close to being on point; but the extraordinary thing is, when they finally located that sub it was less than a quarter of a mile from the group's average.

If we take lots of independent estimates and we find that they can yield information better than any one participant can generate; if we can find a way to mix them together, we can get a good result. Nobody was able to steer others away from their analysis; errors wouldn't be compounded or created by the most aggressive arguer; the results were impersonal, they were independent, and more than that: They were accurate. That naval officer had created a technology to overcome ignorance and the high costs of information.

That, I think, is much of what's behind economists' affinity for markets. They think that markets do what that naval experiment did: They provide an inexpensive, accurate, and valuable way to take lots and lots of information and compress it into a clear and accessible form. In this case, price; economists think prices are primarily a system of information. They're condensed information; and having access to prices, they significantly lower the cost and simultaneously create accurate incentives. Remember, it's in prices that Smith's "invisible hand" finds the information to guide its action;

and when the prices are wrong, the action is wrong. Markets are a human invention that ranks right up there with the wheel and control of fire.

Economists like markets so much they sometimes create artificial markets to see if they can find a way to reveal the wisdom of the crowd. The University of Iowa for several years has run something called the Iowa Electronic Markets, and they use that to predict election outcomes, to predict changes in Federal Reserve Policy, or even something as trivial as the opening weekend box office take when a new movie opens. The way it works is they create futures contracts that people buy with real money that cover different potential outcomes. If people think an event is likely to happen, the price of the contract goes up; and if they think it's less likely to happen, the price of the contract is likely to go down. Whenever they have information, they can compare it to the group's current average that's found in the price of the contract and see whether or not they think they have information that will change that.

The value of the contract is really the collective bet of all the market participants. Here's an example; here's how this works: Say it's a presidential election, and let's say that the Republican candidate is elected. Holders of future contracts for the Republican can redeem them for a dollar a piece. The Democratic nominee contracts, having not been elected, have a redemption value of zero. Before the election, there's this active market as people all over the country acquire information anywhere from any source that makes them believe the chances of one candidate are improving; they see a profit opportunity by quickly trying to buy those contracts, and that increased action drives the price upward. Of course, if information anywhere in the system leads people to believe a candidate's chances of election are being reduced, then they want to get out now before the price falls; and, of course, selling those contracts drives down the price. Price changes reflect any change in information anywhere almost instantly. New polls take days to conduct and process. But election markets respond immediately; people watch them and see what happens on an hour-by-hour basis. It's important: The "investors" are not buying and selling contracts based on their preference for candidates; if you want to make money, you have to reveal the truth. You invest in contracts for the candidate your information tells you is most likely to win; it's not a preference poll, it's an information evaluation poll. Over several election cycles, the Iowa Electronic Markets have consistently predicted the actual vote with more accuracy than the major polls. It's Surowieki's wisdom of crowds in action; it's a mechanism that produces vast quantities of useful information cheaply and accessibly.

Collectively, we know more than we do individually. Economists are awfully good at thinking about things like this; we aren't always so good at thinking about how other people are going to view our own thinking. Buoyed by the successes of the Iowa Electronics experiment, the Pentagon a few years ago came up with a plan for a Terrorism Futures Market. Anyone, anywhere in the world, could buy futures contracts on specific terrorist events and time frames. For example, if a subway bombing in New York City occurs before August 12, there's a payoff; if it doesn't, the futures contract falls to zero. The idea the Pentagon had was that if people anywhere in the crowd, in the world, had any information that led them to believe that such an attack was likely, the price of the futures contract would rise; if they had information that it was less likely, it would fall; and the Pentagon planners thought they could use changes in price in the Terrorism Futures Market as a very low-cost intelligence evaluation and prediction process.

Technically, they were probably right; but talk about a public relations disaster. The angry speeches on the floor of Congress, the media columns that were generated, the talking heads on television: all of them were horrified. Make a monetary profit off a national disaster? Bet on a tragedy? That felt like it was, and probably even was, morally wrong. There was also some fear that economic thinking might be affecting terrorists in the whole process. People argued that if you bought futures contracts on events you were actually planning, then when you carried them out you'd end up with a financial windfall as a result of being a terrorist. The massive opposition to that market was overwhelming; it was never implemented. Being able to think like an economist is not always a highly appreciated trait.

Prices can give us a lot of important information about the wisdom of the crowd, but sometimes we need information that price alone isn't enough to carry. We may want information on specific qualities, and perhaps we may need that information a lot; and there are some other insights to be offered in there as well. One of the things that all of us care about is the crashworthiness of the automobiles we drive. If my family is unnecessarily harmed because I made the wrong choice of car, I think that would be catastrophic. I could buy one of each model car and then crash it into a wall, I think that would be a lot of fun; but it's probably prohibitively expense. That is valuable information for me, but it's not going to justify that kind of a cost; I can't produce that for myself. Are there incentives for someone else to do that for me? That's a complicated question. Information isn't like an ice cream cone; if one person consumes it, it's not gone, it's not unavailable to others, it's not used up. Information used by one can be equally valuable to other people.

Is that a good thing or a bad thing? The kind of smart aleck answer, of course, is yes, it's a good thing and a bad thing. It's good because there's a potential for us to divide up that extraordinary cost, produce it once, and then share it and use it many, many times, over and over. The shared cost for each of us will be less than the combined benefit will be, and we'll be able to afford doing that; a Pareto improvement is possible. The unfortunate part of that is that collecting that information is kind of like cleaning up the atmosphere: Everybody wants the information, but nobody really wants to have to pay for it; we all want to ride for free. If I can wait and get enough others to chip in and pay for the crash test results, I get them for nothing. I'm better off if I don't pay. I also know that if many others do not step up, then even if I contribute a huge amount, the tests won't get done. I have to find some other way to find out this information. Of course, voluntary cooperation among 250 million Americans is no more likely to work here than it did in solving global climate change. Could an entrepreneur, somebody get rich, by conducting these tests and then selling the results over and over again? Maybe, but there are real obstacles; because once those first few sales are made, that reusable information is impossible to control. It's like air in a balloon: One leak, it's out into the atmosphere, it's free for all, and the profit potential has disappeared.

Yet information on crash worthiness does get generated; it's made available to the public free of charge. Who has an incentive to do that? Actually, there are two sets of crash test data that get generated. The first is produced by the National Highway Traffic Safety Administration, and we know how they solve the free rider problem: They don't let us ride for free; we have to pay those costs in compulsory taxes. But more interestingly, there's a second group, and that's the Insurance Institute for Highway Safety. I'm going to tell you that they are benefited by getting all that expensive information and then giving it away for free. Think like an economist: Their profits get reduced when people drive less crashworthy cars; safer cars mean lower claims, they mean higher profits. The more information and the better the information that's in consumers' hands, the higher the insurance company's profits. The more consumers who have that information, the more the profits will be increased; and how do you get the widest distribution possible on information? You make it free.

There's one final technological innovation I want to talk about briefly; a way we come up with to lower the costs of acquiring information, to increase the amount of optimal information. We've already developed a lot of transactions that take place between experts. People will acquire very specialized knowledge, and then we enter into what's called the principal-agent relationship. We're going to pay somebody more knowledgeable than ourselves to make important decisions for us; hopefully they'll have our interests foremost. An obvious case of this is diagnostic physicians. It's only when I'm finding myself in dire need of medical knowledge that it becomes important enough to me to figure out what's going wrong. But a wrong diagnosis at that time, a wrong decision, can be very costly. I don't know ahead of time which knowledge I'll need to treat what disease and what condition. When you begin having chest pains and shortness of breath, it's too late to start applying to medical school. Instead, we turn to experts who are going to do this for us.

To become a medical doctor is an extremely expensive proposition. I know this because I married my wife a month before she started medical school, and I have two children who've gone through medical school. It's an extremely expensive proposition. It probably is an investment of a million dollars or more when you count in the opportunity costs of time; and it's really only worth it to make that investment because the information that doctors have isn't like crash test data. No one can sell it over and over again; they have to have individually tailored information to give to the patient that matches their immediate need. The extraordinary costs of capturing that tremendous investment are possible only because the diagnosis that you gave to the last patient is of absolutely no value to me; I'm going to have to buy my own. I want the doctor to evaluate my EKG, not the last patient's; and I can't resell my EKG tracing to someone else. The next patient's going to have to buy her own personal diagnosis.

So where are we now? Complete ignorance is certainly not bliss. It leads to bad decisions, often with harsh consequences. On the other hand, complete omniscience is neither humanly possible nor affordable. Information is limited, information is costly. The human dilemma then is to navigate rationally between these two extremes, balancing the costs of making wrong decisions with the costs of acquiring more information.

What, in the final analysis, does that mean for you? It means that the amount of investment in the information you make rationally is going to depend on the size of the cost if you make a wrong decision. It means that when information is widely scattered and diffusely held, you can look for processes, like markets, that are going to aggregate and compress the information to see if it will reveal the wisdom of a crowd. But before placing too much faith in the wisdom of a crowd, you want to ask yourself: Is this a situation where there are multiple people making truly independent evaluations, or is this a structure where each is just repeating what others have said; they must be independent evaluations. Is each person's interest best served by revealing their best estimate; would it be mis-served by a systematic distortion? In the Iowa Electronic Markets, when people had information they thought changed the likelihood of an outcome, they could only profit from that if they revealed that information in their market behavior. Finally, expert advice reduces the costs of overcoming ignorance, but only if it's truly in the expert's best interest to disseminate complete and unbiased information. Is it in the insurance industry's best interest to tell you the truth about the crashworthiness of cars? Probably it is. Is it in the doctor's best interest to tell you the truth about your diagnosis? Probably it is. Is it the used car salesman's best interest to tell you the truth about the cars on his lot? Probably not. As always, economic thinking involves a consideration of incentives; yours and everyone else's. That's true whether we're talking about actions, and it's true when we're talking about information.

This is a lot of information about the economics of information; but there's more. In the next lecture, we're going to ask a slightly different question:

What's the rational thing to do when what we know is unknowable; when chance and risk are going to lead to a future that it is impossible to predict with certainly. There are unavoidable elements of that, and it's an important choice. That's the topic we'll take up next time.

Playing the Odds—Reason in a Risky World
Lecture 7

We would like to know some future event is going to come out in certainty. Some cases are absolutely unknowable. If you spent your entire fortune gathering data on coin flipping—you got data information on the mass of coins, on rotational forces, on wind velocity, on the bounce response from different surfaces—no matter how much information you got, you would never know for certain what's going to happen the next time you flip that coin. ... It depends on chance; there's unavoidable risk.

You can never be too safe, right? It may surprise you to know that in thinking like an economist, there is such a thing as being too safe. Every increase in safety has its cost, if not in dollars then in opportunity cost. Diminishing marginal value and rising marginal cost dictate that at some point, adding a little more safety is not going to justify the rising cost of achieving it.

This doesn't sound right—isn't a human life priceless? Individuals actually decide the value of their safety every day. Every time we drive a car or walk across a street, we risk harm and death. The fact that we do it means that we rationally decide that we value getting to the destination enough to justify undertaking that risk. Whenever public policy issues are under consideration, economists see that we must put some measurable value on human lives, at least in a statistical sense. We could choose to live in hermetically sealed bubbles, but it would cost us too much—not just in terms of money, but in terms of the experiences we'd have to give up. There are some aspects of life that we cherish even more than a bit more safety.

The concept of safety extends to the various risks we face in life: That car you bought might be a lemon; the retirement portfolio you've been building for 30 years could go broke. In a world where everything affects everything else, where some consequences and influences are always unknowable, and where no one is in control, there will always be **risks**. We can try to understand and manage them, but we can't eliminate them.

So what is the smart thing to do when faced with a decision that involves risk? Economists use a concept called **expected value**. Expected value conceptually is what would happen if we could replay decisions over and over again. It gives us the average outcome, even though in reality we may only be making this decision one time. To find the expected value, simply take the **probability** of each possible outcome, multiply that by the value of the outcome, and add all of these values together. Knowing the expected value helps you make a rational decision.

John Howard/Digital Vision/Thinkstock.

Many decisions involve inescapable, probabilistic risks.

But a lot of probabilities in our lives cannot be calculated exactly. What are the chances that my house is going to catch fire or that my car will be stolen? I can only estimate those probabilities using historical data. For example, the risk of dying in a hurricane in the United States in any given year is about 1 in 6 million, but I can guess that if I live in the Midwest my risk is lower, and if I live along the Gulf of Mexico it is higher. The whole idea of thinking like an economist means being ever cognizant of your incentives and those of others. Do not be misled by other people's interpretation of risk, which will not necessarily mesh with yours. Also, keep in mind that our knowledge of probabilities can be systematically distorted. When there's a lot of group interaction, the people making decisions feed off each other. Rationally ignorant people (i.e., all of us) are susceptible to **information cascades** that can lead us wildly astray. These include events like stock market crashes and the dot-com tech bubble in the 1990s. Many of the decisions we make in life involve inescapable, probabilistic risks. It is up to us to estimate carefully both the probabilities and the payouts from various outcomes. ∎

expected value: Formally, it is the sum of the payoffs from all possible outcomes, each multiplied by the probability of its occurrence. In essence, it is the average outcome that would result from repeating the same decision multiple times.

information cascade: A growing group assessment of a situation where all members are uninformed of actual facts but form opinions based on the number of others who assert something to be true. Once this process has begun, people still undecided about the truth of the proposition in question view each new adherent as evidence of the proposition's truth.

probability: The probability of any event (e.g., getting heads in a coin toss) is 1 divided by the number of total possible outcomes. In the case of a coin toss, the probability of heads is 1/2.

risk: The degree to which an outcome depends on probability because future events cannot be perfectly predicted.

Take-Away Points

1. When making decisions involving outcomes that will be determined by chance, the best "bet" is determined by the expected value of each option. Expected value, in turn, is determined by the probability of each possible outcome and the payoff or consequence should that outcome occur.

2. Comparing the expected value of alternatives aids in rational decision making. When the expected value of a total-loss collision for an older car becomes less than the cost of insurance to cover it, it becomes rational to cancel that coverage.

Playing the Odds—Reason in a Risky World

Lecture 7—Transcript

"You can never too safe!" Is there a mother anywhere that has not ended the conversation with one of her children by saying just exactly that? You should probably pity the mother of economists, because you know exactly what they're going to say: "Actually, Mom, you can be too safe." That's really the topic we're going to get into today in Lecture 7 in our series on "How to Think Like an Economist." We're going to explore the reasoning behind that conclusion that an economist would reach, that there is such a thing as being too safe. You know basically the reason for that: If there's no such thing as a free lunch, there's no such thing as "free safety" either. Every increase in safety has its cost, if not in dollars at least in opportunity cost. We also know that with diminishing marginal value and rising marginal cost, at some point to be just a little safer, adding a little more safety, is not going to justify the rising cost of achieving it. Like ignorance, there's an optimal level of risk and there's an optimal level of safety.

The question to start with is: How much safety is too much? How much risk is too little? If we remain consistent to the position we've adopted, the one we borrowed from Pareto, then individuals get to decide for themselves what is the value of safety to them; no outsider, no economist, no other person can decide what should matter most to them or how much. But every single time you get in an automobile and drive somewhere, or you cross a street upon which others are driving, you do take a risk of harm and death; and yet we do it willingly. If we believe in rationality, that in itself is proof that we must value getting to the destination enough to justify undertaking that risk.

Whenever public policy issues are under consideration, economists think we must—we have to—put some measurable value on a human lives, at least in a statistical sense. If we're going to drill a tunnel through a mountain, there's a high likelihood that someone will die in the process, and we must decide whether or not it's worth it. I made that argument in class once, and I got a very heated response from a student. He said, "The value of human life is infinite!" I think he was really talking about his own human life; but in general, he was making that argument. But I said to him, "I'm not putting a value on your life, you are." So I asked him, "How'd you get here this morning?" He said, "I drove." I said, "What did you drive?" He listed some small, old car appropriate for a limited student budget. I said, "You should have come in an armored personnel carrier; you can get them on surplus from the U.S. government, and you would have been much safer if you'd done that." He said what you would have said: "That's absurd." But then I said to him that "The reduced risk of driving in that carrier apparently was not worth the cost to you, and I rest my case. You don't value your life as highly as you thought you did."

There the conversation just lapsed into contemplative silence; but our own behavior proves over and over again that we do evaluate ourselves at times as being too safe, and that's true whenever the cost of reducing or eliminating the risk becomes too high. I suppose we could live in hermetically sealed bubbles and bombproof bunkers underground and we could lead long lives; but literally, those would be lives not worth living. It would cost us too much, not just in terms of money, but in terms of all the experiences we'd have to give up. There certainly are some aspects of life that we cherish even more than a bit more safety. Many of the things that give life its meaning come with risks. You can be much too safe.

Safety isn't just about fatal risks or grievous bodily harm; that reasoning applies to all the various risks we face in life. That car that you just bought might turn out to be a lemon; the retirement plan where you've been putting your money for the last 30 years could go broke; the house that you built so carefully could burn down; that career choice you made could turn out badly. All of those are risks we take; in a world in which everything affects everything else, where some consequences and influences are always unknowable, where no one is in control, there will always be risks. It makes sense for us to understand them, to manage them, to contain them, but it's beyond the realm of practicality or even wisdom to imagine eliminating them. The issue is: How do you live with risks? We're going to talk about that today.

Economists tend to distinguish two things when they're in this kind of an area of discussion: the first one is uncertainty and the other one is risk. Uncertainty for economists refers to a situation where the information we have is incomplete; and that was the topic of the last lecture. Of course, uncertainty I guess in one sense can be cured by having more and better information; we would be more accurately able to predict the future. If we had perfect information, uncertainty would be eliminated. But, of course, last time we found out that to try and have perfect information would be irrationally expensive.

Today what I want to talk about is thinking like an economist about the other source of the future's unknowability: This is a situation that economists call "risk." There are places where we could have more and more and more information, and we still wouldn't be able to know what we really want to know. We would like to know some future event is going to come out in certainty. Some cases are absolutely unknowable. If you spent your entire fortune gathering data on coin flipping— you got data information on the mass of coins, on rotational forces, on wind velocity, on the bounce response from different surfaces—no matter how much information you got, you would never know for certain what's going to happen the next time you flip that coin. If you try to predict the outcome from a large number of coin flips, even with all the information available to you, you're going to be wrong half the time. That's the kind of event that is marked by randomness. The certainty about that outcome is impossible; it's what we call "probabilistic." It depends on chance; there's unavoidable risk.

What is the smart thing to do when faced with a decision that involves this kind of risk? Faced with probabilistic decisions, economists used this formalized concept that goes under the name of "expected value." Economists know that life is not like a video game; there's not a redo button, there's not a play over game, there's not a chance to redo it time and time again when we face situations of risk. But what expected value is conceptually is what would happen if we could replay decisions over and over and over again? What would be the average outcome if we remade the decision and experienced its consequences time and time again; what would be the average result?

To find the expected value, you need a couple of things: You need to know the probability of each possible outcome, and you need to be able to multiply that by the value of the outcome, and then add them all up. We'll try it in a minute to make sure you understand what I'm saying. It sounds like it's complicated, but it really isn't that hard to do, as long as you really know the probabilities and you know the payoffs.

Our purpose in this course is really to focus mostly on the conceptual vision of economic thinking. I don't think any of us wants to do a lot of problem sets or work through a number of quantitative examples; but I'm going to go through one simple example, just for the purpose of trying to make these concepts a little bit clearer for us. First what we have to do: What is the official, formal mathematical definition of "probability." Formally, the probability of any event—such as flipping heads, rolling a three on a die—is that possible outcome divided by the total number of possible outcomes. You flip a coin, how many possibilities are there? Two; heads is one of the two, so the probability of coming up heads is 1/2; ½ or .5. I'll leave it to you to figure out that it's also the probability of flipping tails. If I were to roll a single die, coming up "3" is one of six possibilities; so the probability of rolling a three is 1/6, or probability of .1667. I'm going to tell you that if I roll that die over and over and over again, I have an extraordinary amount of confidence that a "3" is going to show up about 1/6 of the time on average. But I'm not very confident about what's going to come up the very next time I roll. Once I know the probabilities, then if I can accurately estimate the value of the outcome, I can calculate expected value.

Let's try it: I'm going to propose a game to you, a really fun game, "heads I win, tails you lose"; I like that kind of a game. Here are the rules: You're going to flip a coin, and if it comes up heads, you pay me $1; if it comes up tails, you pay me $.50. Sound like a good game to you? I like it. If you do that over and over and over, half the time I'm going to win $1, and half the time I'm going to win $.50. But my average winnings and your average loss will be $.75 cents per coin flip. At no flip at all are $.75 cents actually going to change hands; but that's the average that takes place. That's nice to know, I suppose, and I don't see any of you saying you really want to play that game with me; and knowing expected value probably didn't have much of an influence on that decision. You don't need a lot of mathematical sophistication to know that the game would be all about losses for you.

Let me make it just a little more useful; let's change the rules of the game. Now suppose I say, "I will pay you $.80 to flip the coin under the rules I just announced." Would you do it then? You would certainly gain $.80 from each coin flip; and what would be the expected value, the average of your losses over the long run? On average, you'd win $.05. If instead I said, "I'll pay you $.70 a coin flip to play this game," you could be pretty sure that over the long run you'd lose a nickel on average. Knowing the expected value lets you know how to make a rational decision in that kind of situation involving risk. Casinos get very rich because they're very good at calculate expected values. A lot of gamblers get very poor very fast because they don't know how to calculate expected values, or they just don't believe the numbers apply to them.

Textbooks are very fond of using examples for probability like a coin flip, a roll of the die, or pulling an ace out of a deck of cards because it's very easy to determine the actual, objective probabilities in cases like that. I suppose there are some places in real life where objective probability can be determined. In my home state, the lottery has a lot of different prizes, and they tell you on the website what the probabilities are. For example, the $175,000 prize coming from a $1 bet happens once in every 135 million tickets. If you go through the numbers—and try it if you want—the expected value per ticket then comes out to be about $.06; people trade a $1 bet for an expected return of $.06. Scratch tickets in my state also: Some of them have a 1 in 1 million chance of getting a $20,000 prize. That's going to come out to an expected value of about $.02. It's a lot like the game I tried to play with you. No lottery ticket ever pays $.02 cents; 999,999 pay nothing; 1 pays $20,000; on average, people get back $.02 for their dollar bet. That's probably the basis behind the bumper sticker that says, "The Lottery is a Tax on People Who are Bad at Math." It's probably also bad news for the one fourth of Americans who polls tells us think that winning the lottery is a viable means of achieving financial security. Maybe those people aren't completely rational; maybe they're just ill-informed.

But there's a lot in our lives that's much more complex than flipping a coin or rolling a die. For a lot of the risks we face in life there really aren't objective probabilities that are well and easily defined. Each event, each participant, and each situation are just a little bit different from the others. I would like to know: What are the chances that my house is going to catch fire; that my car is the one that's going to be stolen; that I'm going to need dentures; or that I'm going to have to spend time in the hospital during the coming year? I can't simply count the sides on a die or the number of cards in a deck in order to calculate those probabilities, so we estimate them using historical data. But I always want to know: Is that directly applicable to me? Is the future going to be the same as the past? Is that the correct comparison? For example, the national risk of dying in a hurricane in any given year in the United States is about 1 in 6 million. But I have to believe that if I live in North Dakota it's not going to be that high, and I have to believe if I live in New Orleans it's going to be higher than that. If I live on high ground my chances are better; if I live below sea level they're probably worse. If I want to know about the probability of dying in a fire—if you take the total number of fire deaths in the U.S. and divide by the population—the average risk of a fire death is about 1 in 91,000. But I'm pretty sure that if I live with a smoker the chances go up, and if I install fire alarms the chances will go down.

Mathematicians can tell us with certainty what the odds are for well-defined games of chance. I wish it was as easy to find out what the real odds are in situations that we live with in the real world; but unfortunately there is uncertainty about probability and risk. We don't have enough information to tell us what the true probabilistic risks are; and that can certainly make applying this concept of expected value more difficult.

I want to give you a personal example of ignorance about consequences; and this is a true and, believe me, profoundly creepy story. We awoke one night last summer with a bat circling around my wife's head. I immediately decided I would be the hero of the hour; I grabbed the tennis racquet, we opened the skylight, and I herded that bat back out into the night. I thought when I climbed back into bed: Adventure done; hero status achieved. Maybe some bad dreams for a couple of nights, but the adventure was over. "Not quite," my wife informed me. She said the state of Massachusetts has a strict protocol: Bats are known to have high incidence of rabies, and they have sharp teeth. If one had bitten us in the hairline while we were asleep, it would have been invisible; it's highly unlikely, the probability was tiny. Not zero, but small. But the state said, "You must be treated for rabies." I said, "Why?" The answer is, of course, the state was calculating expected value. Certainly the probability of exposure was small; but the consequences of being wrong would have been sure, certain, and painful death. There is no cure for rabies once contracted. That's a payoff I did not want to incur, I very much wished to avoid. I did my own expected value calculations and I agreed with the state; we got the shots.

Let's review some of the things we've talked about: Remember, the whole idea of thinking like an economist means that you're going to be ever-cognizant of your own incentives and the incentives that others have. I thought maybe we'd take a moment and look at an example of thinking about different incentives for different players in situations of risk. The example I want to talk about is the way in which hedge fund managers get compensated as they manage funds. In recent times, there's been a relatively large movement of people shifting—particularly wealthy people—some of their funds into hedge funds. These are funds that are not publicly traded; the rules are you can only take your money out at preset intervals. You're turning over control to a professional manager, and originally they used a lot of complex strategies to buy some of this to hedge against inflation and some of that to hedge against market movements; but in general, their private investment funds are professionally managed.

It's in the compensation formula where it's interesting to think like an economist. The standard in the United States today is what they call "2 and 20," and that means there's a fee of 2 percent on the amount of money involved, plus the manager gets 20 percent of any games that he or she can generate. But it's kind of a one-way street: The manager does not share in any losses; and that means, of course, that the manager's payoffs are really different from those of his clients. Here's a hypothetical example: Suppose you had a million dollars invested in a hedge fund, and the manager's considering two possible investments. One of them is a risky investment; there's a 50 percent chance it'll gain a half million and a 50 percent chance it will lose a half million. The other alternative is to hold a safe one million dollar investment. Your choices: Hold a million, or take a coin flip bet that you can gain or lose half a million dollars.

Pop quiz, let's review: What's the expected value of return on this risky investment? It's .5 times $500,000, which is +$250,000; and .5 times a loss of $500,000, which is -$250,000, and that's total flat zero. Maybe you like the thrill; maybe you like to gamble; but in a probabilistic sense, the expected value of return on that investment is zero. You can either have the zero return safe investment or zero expected value risky investment, that's your option. Let's think about the manager: The manager keeps the money in the safe, $1 million asset; he gets a $2,000 fee for managing the money (two percent of your million). But if he puts money in the risky investment, his expected value is not 0, his expected value is +$52,000. Why? If the investment pays off—and there's a 50 percent change it will—he'll get 2 percent of 1.5 million (that's $3,000), plus 20 percent of the gain of half a million (that's $100,000); so if it pays off, he gets $103,000. If the investment loses—and there's a 50 percent chance it will—his fee falls down to $1,000, and 2 percent of that is from the remaining half million. His expected value is $52,000, and yours was 0. That means the manager has an incentive to take on quite a bit more risks than many of his clients might deem wise.

Understanding this concept of Expected Value helps us define our own optimal strategies when we face risks; and that's an important part of thinking like an economist. Using it to anticipate how others, like the hedge fund manager, will behave is at least as valuable as figuring out how we should behave.

Let's return to a new wrinkle in considering the difficulties that arise from uncertainty about risks. It's not hard to see the usefulness of this Expected Value concept, but the actual values of probabilities or payoffs can be very difficult to figure out, and they're not precisely known. Even worse, there's ample evidence that our knowledge of them can be systematically distorted, partly by our own psychological processes.

Remember we talked before about the wisdom of crowds in a book by James Surowieki? Today I want to talk about the foolishness of crowds. There's a subfield in economics that really comes out of psychology; we call it "behavioral economics." We'll return to that in more detail in Lecture 11. But it spends a lot of time looking at perceptions and how they're formed. In Surowieki's book, he talked about doing experiments, estimating the number of jelly beans in a jar; and he told that unique story of finding a lost submarine by averaging the independent predictions of multiple experts. But what was crucial in that, remember? Each individual had to come up with an independent estimate or conclusion. They couldn't confer, they couldn't share ideas, they couldn't push each other to conclusions; it was independent conclusions that got aggregated, and that led to the wisdom of the crowd. When we compare that to what we find in a lot of the psychological evidence: When there's a lot of group interaction, when the people who are making decisions are feeding off each other, we're as likely to cascade off into a madness of crowds rather than a wisdom of crowds. Rationally ignorant people—and remember, we're all rationally ignorant—are susceptible to what are called "information cascades" that can lead us all wildly astray.

How about a hypothetical? I try to keep my children healthy, and so I decide that I want to feed them apples, apple juice, and applesauce as alternatives to some of the junk snacks that are so popular these days. Let's suppose that apple growers, in order to try and reduce their costs, have found that there's a chemical that will just make all the apples ripen at the same time so that it's cheaper to harvest. I really don't know anything about this, I'm pretty sure I couldn't pronounce its chemical name if I had to. I have no idea if it rapidly breaks down; I have no idea if there's any residue in what my children eat; I have no idea if it has potential carcinogenic properties. But someone, anyone, makes a public assertion that they have figured out that the chemical poses a significant risk of harm to my children; I have no way to evaluate that claim. Remember, I'm rationally ignorant. The assertion itself seems to me to be evidence that somebody must know something that I don't know; somebody must know that there are harmful effects. Then if a second person comes, and persuaded by the first says, "Yes, I, too, believe there are harmful effects," I know that I'm ignorant of the facts; I don't know if they are. But if a third, and a fourth, and a fifth are moved by the evidence, the evidence that two other people think there's a risk, then it's more and more likely it's going to make sense for me to assume they know something I don't know; and a social information cascade may follow. Each new adherent to the assertion becomes new evidence that it's true, and I have no grounds to publically challenge that. The conclusion of the crowd is based on the cascade, and I dare not conclude that the probability of harm from that chemical is not something I should be concerned about. After all, everyone knows it's harmful simply because an ever-growing number of people seem to know it.

I've been misleading you; I've tricked you. That really wasn't a hypothetical. In 1989, the chemical I'm talking about was sold under the common name of Alar; and a public interest group released a study saying that they had concluded that this was a highly dangerous chemical. You know how the media are: Once this was out, the media reported on it over and over again. *60 Minutes* made it the lead story and put a skull and crossbones behind the correspondent to emphasize the danger. Hearing all of that, there were harsh congressional hearings on the floor of the Congress and the Senate; movie stars wept tears saying, "Save our children"; and Alar was removed from the market. Polls in America showed that the American people thought it was one of the major risks to their children's health. Years later, American Medical Association, having looked carefully at the actual data said, "When used in the approved, regulated fashion, as it was, Alar does not pose a risk to the public's health." But the hard evidence came long after that information cascade had fed on itself; a "fact" had become true simply because so many people came to believe it. Rationally ignorant people, reinforcing each other's subjective and inaccurate estimates of risk, collectively led to a result that was really foolishness, and it came from the crowd.

Cascades like that feed financial panics and bubbles. I think one of the most famous was what's known as the "Dutch Tulip Mania" in the 1630s. There was a wild cascade at that time: Tulips had just been developed, and the value of a single bulb rose higher and higher, seemingly without limit. They're lovely flowers, but there's no logical reason why a tulip bulb should cost more than a house; it seems irrational. By the end of the tulip bulb bubble, the price of a single bulb cost several times an average working man's annual salary. But everyone "knew" what a great investment they were; and they were a great investment, the price just kept rising. Until it began to fall; and what cascades up, can cascade down. Others sell, and they again know something I don't know; I better sell, too. The panic was fed with the same kind of information that inflated the bubble.

In the nearly four centuries since, we've seen all kinds of bubbles and bursts: There was the 1987 stock market crash; there was the "irrational exuberance" of the dot com tech bubble in the 1990s; and, of course, the housing price inflation that preceded the financial crash of 2008. There have been bubbles like these all over the world, and they result from three things: rational ignorance, unavoidable risk, and our own susceptibility to information cascades. Those are three of the things we've been talking about in this course.

What should you take away from all of this? Many of the decisions we make in life really involve inescapable, probabilistic risks. The rational approach to those decisions really means we have to take the time to estimate carefully both the probabilities and the payouts from various outcomes. With those, we can think in terms of expected value, a sort of a benchmark to help us decide: At what point do you forego comprehensive insurance on that aging clunker? What's a reasonable price to pay for an extended warranty on the new furnace? Should you buy the trip insurance when you book the cruise? Which investment portfolio is the best one to fund your future retirement? Is exploratory surgery a wise choice? Of course, most important of all, should you get rabies shots if you awake with a bat in your bedroom? It's also important to remember that in most real world cases, the expected values we actually use are going to be dependent on subjective probabilities, and those can be systematically distorted by "experts" whose interests diverge from our own—as in the case of the hedge funds—or by social cascades, when we're pushed to irrational exuberance or even irrational gloom.

We have one more step to go in our examination of ignorance, risk, and information. Most of the information we need or want starts out in the possession of other people; and if we think like economists we know they're going to respond to their incentives, they're going to use that information strategically. In a very real sense, then, that's what makes knowledge into power. That's the topic of our next lecture.

The Economics of Information
Lecture 8

You can see that [the financial crisis of 2008]—the rise and the fall, the bubble and the burst—are really reflections of information asymmetry, rational ignorance, and risk. Far too many of us accepted a financial blind date, forgetting how easily trust can be misplaced; not because everybody we deal with is inherently dishonest, but because, just like us, everyone we deal with faces inevitable uncertainty, ignorance, and risk. When we forget that is when we collectively get into some real trouble.

Because we are rationally ignorant, we have to get most of our information from others. This opens the door for other people to use information strategically. Anytime you have a decision to make that's going to affect somebody else, and that person has information relevant to your decision, that person has an incentive to filter, distort, obfuscate, subsidize, or hide some of the information to influence your decision in a way that will benefit them. People know that altering the composition and quality of the information they give to others can probably influence the other's choice; in fact, it would be irrational of them not to alter the information.

George Akerlof shared the 2001 Nobel Prize in Economics in part for examining the social consequences of **information asymmetry**. Here is a summary of his analysis: Who knows how dependable a used car is going to be? The current owner; he has years of experience with it. He's much more likely to get rid of an undependable car but keep a good one. The result is, according to Akerlof, that problem cars will probably be overrepresented in the used car market. Buyers don't have any way of knowing how effective an individual car is because there's information asymmetry. Potential buyers, if they assume that sellers are rational, must expect most of the cars to be lemons. So buyers will use expected value analysis and be unwilling to pay a price that's appropriate for a gem of a car, because if it was a gem, why would the owner be trying to sell it? And of course, actual owners of gems won't be willing to sell at a lemon price.

The average quality of used cars on the market fulfills the expectations that they're all going to be lemons. The seller has information the buyer needs, but he can't be trusted to reveal it. Potentially advantageous trades go unmade, and the market breaks down. Everybody behaves rationally, but everybody loses. Buyers disproportionately end up with lemons, and sellers of gems can't get the price they deserve. The result is something that economists call **adverse selection**. The gems are selected out of the market, and only the lemons remain.

Buyers of used cars face the problem of information asymmetry.

Maybe we need a "hostage." In medieval times, when a rival to a sitting king felt he had to signal his own trustworthiness, he might leave his son in the king's castle to be held as a hostage. Then if the rival broke the promise and invaded the king's realm, the king would at least have an opportunity for vengeance if not for direct resistance. The rival had changed his own payoffs from an invasion. Modern warranties are really just hostages; they follow the same reasoning. You know that the car you are selling is a gem. If you offer to pay 50% of any necessary repairs over the first 90 days, that's a credible assertion that your car is not a lemon. Another seller's unwillingness to offer a warranty is credible information that her car is a lemon. That creates an incentive for the owners of disproportionate asymmetric information to reveal it accurately through the use of a warranty.

How do we apply this information? First, we must remember that our inevitable ignorance makes information strategic. Second, we must approach all cases of information asymmetry with a healthy dose of skepticism. If something sounds too good to be true, it probably is. ∎

adverse selection: When the incentives in a situation result in the elimination of the best alternatives, leaving only less desirable options (e.g., when uncertainty about quality drives the best used cars from the market, leaving the lemons).

information asymmetry: A situation in which one party to a transaction has access to information not available, but important, to another party.

Take-Away Points

1. Because a certain degree of ignorance is always rational, there is always the potential for others to use the information they possess to try to influence our choices. Whether called the blind date principle or information asymmetry, this can result in distorted and suboptimal decisions.

2. Rationality dictates that we be ever conscious of the incentives for those from whom we acquire information. Do their ultimate objectives align, or conflict, with our own? Can we create mechanisms or a "hostage," such as a warranty, that would make it in their own interest to reveal their information to us truthfully?

The Economics of Information
Lecture 8—Transcript

Welcome back to the eighth lecture in our series on "How to Think Like an Economist." For the last couple of lectures, we've been thinking like economists about questions of rational decision-making when we have less than perfect information. We've concerned ourselves with issues of uncertainty; we've concerned ourselves with issues of risk. But today I want to take this consideration of rational ignorance into a different area, because we are rationally ignorant, and that opens the door for other people to use information strategically; and after all, most of the information we get, we get from other people. Do you remember the old caution that I'm sure your mother shared with you at some times? "Consider the source." What's in it for him? What incentives does she have to use the information in her control to further her own ends? I want to begin today by just talking in general terms about strategic use of information and the consequences that has for individuals and for social outcomes; and then finally, I want to take a last part of the lecture and an extended look at an example, the so-called "Great Crash of '08," and look at it as a failure of information above all else.

Back in Lecture 6 when we started talking about information, I suggested that metaphorically we think about information as if it was a giant pile of sand. We can go and pick it up, but it is heavy and awkward to carry so we get it in bits and pieces, a bucketful at a time. We could go back for more again and again, but as we acquired additional information, the marginal value of another little bit would decline; we'd hit diminishing returns. At some point, another trip wasn't worth the cost; and that's what determined for us our level of rational ignorance. But you and I know that information is not just lying on the ground waiting to be picked up; mostly, someone else has it. So when we take that metaphorical trip to the information stand, what we're going to find is that some of the "owners" may decide to hide some of it from us; others may offer to carry it home for us for free; or some may simply disguise it, distort it to change its true character. They have incentives to use the information under their control to try and influence our decisions; and, in fact, it would be irrational of them not to that, and it would be unwise of us not to recognize that incentive for them. It's time for us to think about our "informants."

Anytime you have a decision to make that's going to affect somebody else, and that person has information relevant to your decision, he or she has this incentive to filter, to distort, to obfuscate, to subsidize, to hide the information. You know and they know that rationality dictates that I'm going to make my decision with partial and imperfect information. If they alter the composition and the quality of the information I have, they can probably influence the choice I make. I ran into this more than once when I was young and single; and in a book I wrote about this many years ago, I called this the "Blind Date Principle," because I'd learned the hard way you can't always trust your friends' account of how good a blind date is going to be.

Let's just suppose that my friend's sister-in-law comes to town, and she doesn't want to have to spend the evening with her so she's trying to get me to take the sister out for an evening's fun and excitement. She'll tell me, truthfully, her sister-in-law has a great sense of humor. She might even show me a flattering and unretouched picture of her (as she looked 25 years ago). She might forget to mention that her sister's coming to town to compete in the national championship as "America's Loudest Hog-Caller." Sometimes the information was free, some of it was distorted, some was withheld; but a conclusion probably would not have reached if I had all the information was the decision that I reached in that case. Even though my carefree bachelor days are long over, you and I both face figurative blind dates every day of our lives.

Commercial advertising is a blind date. Job interviews are blind dates on both sides, both the job applicant and the employer. Do you remember Anthony Downs's analysis of voters' rational ignorance? Let me tell you, politics is a blind date. Do you recall his conclusion that if you examine the benefits of becoming an informed voter and you compare that to the cost of becoming an informed voter, it's irrational for most of us to gather much political information? But the candidates, they have lots of information about themselves, they have a very significant interest in how we cast our ballots, and the result, of course is that political campaigns are nothing but blind date proposals in the extreme. Candidates spend extraordinary amounts of money trying to change the stock of information we have that's favorable to themselves, and with negative ads to increase the amount of information that's unfavorable to their opponents. It's clear to anyone with a television set that the most effective form of "blind date persuasion" in that kind of a situation is to present the information in a way that's hard to avoid. If you take that 30-second political ad and you put it just before the climactic scene in a popular TV drama, no one will dare change the channel. If you stick it in during a timeout in the final moments of the big game, no one's going to dare leave the room. I often think at the end of an election the greatest social benefit is not that policy's been determined, not that our votes have been counted, but what I find is the greatest advantage of the end of a campaign is those repetitive, non-informative, often insulting and deceptive ads are finally off the air.

George Akerlof shared the 2001 Nobel Prize in Economics in part for taking a more formal approach to what I was calling the "Blind Date Principle." Akerloff spent a lot of time focusing on the social consequences of situations like that; I was, of course, thinking about the individual consequences for myself in a blind date. Unlike me, he didn't call this as a blind date problem; and that may be he had a less traumatic adolescence than I did. Anyway, he decided to use a more formal term, and he called this "information asymmetry"; a situation where one party to a potential interaction has a lot more relevant information than another party. The title of his analysis was *The Market for Lemons*; and in short, here's how it goes: Who knows how dependable a used car is going to be? The answer is: the current owner; they have months, years, of possible experience with it. The presumption is that they're going to be much more likely to get rid of an undependable car; they'll want to dump a lemon and hold onto a gem. The result is, according to Akerloff, that problem cars will be probably be overrepresented in the used car market. Buyers, of course, don't have any way of knowing how effective an individual car is going to be; there's information asymmetry. They don't know that something is a lemon because they don't have the current owner's long-term experience. If they assume sellers are rational, potential buyers are going to assume that most of the cars in the market are lemons Then, of course, they're going to use the expected value analysis we did last time, and buyers should be unwilling to pay a price that's appropriate for a gem, because if it was a gem, why would the owner be trying to sell it? Of course, actual owners of gems won't be willing to sell at a lemon price.

The average quality of cars in the market fulfills the expectations that they're all going to be lemons. The seller has information the buyer needs, but can't be trusted to reveal it. Potentially advantageous trades will go unmade; the market breaks down; everybody behaves rationally, but everybody loses. Buyers disproportionately end up with lemons; sellers of gems can't get the price they deserve. The result of this information asymmetry is something that economists call "adverse selection." The gems are selected out of the market, and the adverse condition is: only the lemons remain.

Maybe it's time for a hostage. In medieval times, when a rival to a sitting king felt he had to signal his own trustworthiness, he might leave his son in the king's castle to be held as a hostage. Then if the rival broke the promise and invaded the king's realm, the king would at least have an opportunity for vengeance if not for direct resistance. Willingness to hold your son as a hostage made the promise credible. The rival had changed his own payoffs from an invasion. This assumes, of course, that there's a strong amount of parental affection; and if you look at the history of royal families, it's possible that if you offered up an overly ambitious son as a hostage and then invaded the king's realm you might actually be solving two problems at once in a fairly clever way.

Modern warranties are really just hostages; they follow the same reasoning, they fill the same purpose. You have a gem; you have the information that shows that your car is a gem. If you bind yourself to paying 50 percent of any necessary repairs over the first 90 days, that's a credible statement that your assertion that your car is not a lemon is true. It distinguishes your car; it signals its own quality. An unwillingness to offer a warranty is credible information that the car is, in fact, some kind of a lemon. That creates an incentive for the owners of disproportionate asymmetric information to reveal it accurately through the use of a hostage like a warranty.

For the past two-and-a-half lectures, we've been thinking like economists about this ubiquitous problem of limited information, and now we've add the idea of strategic resources to uncertainty and risk. Those are important concerns, and they're insights that matter when, as individuals, we go shopping for a used car. But they're also so fundamental that when those concepts are misunderstood, when these problems arise, entire economic systems the world over can be shaken to the brink by the kind of situation we've been talking about. What I want to do for the rest of the time we have today is to use our analysis of the economics of information, and use it as a key to try and understand an important event, what we call the "Great Financial Crash of '08" and the serious recession that followed it.

As you'll recall, in the very first decade of the 21st century, there was an economic and financial crisis of proportions that hadn't been felt since the 1930s. Households and nations both fell into serious difficulty; and it all reached a head, sort of a crisis, in a financial panic: a world-wide credit market freeze in the fall of 2008. The financial system for a few days at least simply stopped. Editorials and pundits all over the world pointed their finger at greed, at irresponsibility, at incompetence, and at criminal fraud; and there were some of all of those in there. But I think it's also true that there was a tremendous amount of uncertainty, rational ignorance, reaction to risk, social cascades, and information asymmetry all coming together in what was a perfect storm of financial crisis. I want to explore that now.

There is consensus among economists that the crisis really began, had its roots, in housing markets, especially in the United States. I want to take a few minutes and talk about housing and housing markets, and talk about finance, and then I'm going to try to draw this together. You know housing is special. It's not like buying a new coat; you're buying a long-lived physical asset that provides shelter, it provides status, it provides location, it allows you access to public benefits, and it lasts years and years into the future. You buy all that in one lump sum up front, and it's expensive. There's sort of a rule of thumb that says you can afford up to two-and-a-half to three times your annual income for housing; but very few of us have enough savings to do that. So the first step in this crisis is: To buy a home, almost all of us have to borrow; and at that point, this physical asset sitting on a lot somewhere becomes entwined with the ethereal world of finance, where values are floating in air and hard to see. Without borrowing, very few of us could buy; and if few can buy—remember those two sides to every transaction?—few can sell, and the whole market freezes up.

Let's begin our analysis of information and the crash of '08 by looking at the fundamental characteristics of any loan. Remember our Foundation

Principles? Each transaction has at least two sides; every dollar that's borrowed is also a dollar lent; and any voluntary transaction, economists believe, both participants think they're going to be better off. A mortgage creates opportunities for gain for both, the borrower and the lender. But it also creates extraordinary amounts of risk. People don't like risk; are there ways to control it? For the lender, the risk clearly is that the borrower will be unable or unwilling to pay back that loan in full or in part; repayment is an uncertain future event. We talked about that last time. The expected value of that event depends on the probability of being fully repaid. But what is that probability? How do you find out that probability? It's not something objective like heads, where you can count there's one side heads and one side tails. There's no clear source of objective information on risks about people's behavior in the future. The lender's going to be, at the end of this process, rationally and necessarily ignorant about the buyer's future. Of course, the buyer's kind of uncertain about his or her own future, too; who isn't?

But there's a serious information asymmetry in this, because even though both of them are uncertain, the borrower knows far more about his own long-term financial prospects, about any impending large expenses, about job and marital security, about their own future health prospects, any potential inheritance or legal liabilities. Rational borrowers may try to set up the lender on—you guessed it—a blind date. Lenders, of course, don't like blind dates; so the lender's going to try and do everything he or she can to protect themselves against that. Historically, in mortgage markets there were requirements of absolute complete disclosure and documentation. A borrower had to prove their financial history; they had to prove their employment status; they had to provide checkable credit references; and the lender would really pay good money to acquire that information. They'd buy and they'd trust the credit histories and the credit scores from the three credit bureaus.

How did the lenders know the credit bureau's information is accurate? Again, thinking like economists, they think about the credit bureau's incentives. The credit bureaus make money only if their data is accurate; and if they start providing inaccurate information, they're going to lose the full value of their database. But even with that, full documentation, full evidence, the reports of credit bureaus, there's still some risk that remains. What's the final defense? The final defense is, as we said before, a hostage, a mortgage lien; because if the borrower fails to pay, you can foreclose on the house, you can sell the house and recapture your funds lent. The risks were controlled for decades with full documentation, required information, plus a hostage of a mortgage lien. That reduced the risk of loss to lenders. It increased the expected value of the loan; and for most of the 20th century, the information demands in mortgage and housing markets kept the number of really bad blind dates fairly low.

Changes in the 1990s and the early 2000s, however, created a whole new set of incentives, it provided for much less information in markets, and created a worldwide crisis. I want to be really honest with you here for just a second. I want you to bear with me for a few moments, because my intent is to see if I can thoroughly confuse you. I want you to find out that you don't have any idea of what I'm talking about; and if you'll trust me, the more confused I make you now, the better you're going to understand my final point in a few moments. The question we need to ask is: Who needs the information about the mortgage, when do they need it, who has it, and how can I get it?

Most loans really originate on a local basis; a local bank or a savings and loan gives cash to a buyer, they buy the house, and it's purchased in their own locality. If the bank keeps it, the originator is the one who gets harmed if there's a future loss. And in knowing that, it has a pretty strong incentive to want that information we talked about, to accurately assess the value of the house. Demand clear and accurate information. But increasingly, there are these expansive secondary markets for mortgages, and what originators do is they'll take the mortgage and they'll sell it to a pension fund, to an insurance company, or some other financial institution. The original bank gets its money back in a matter of days or weeks; it makes some money in proceeds from the fees in creating the mortgage instrument, but when it sells it all the risk goes to the buyer of the mortgage. For the bank, it's the salability rather than the long-term performance of the loan that matters. The bank gets paid when the loan is made, not when it's repaid.

If salability depends on having this full documentation and having an accurate assessment of the market value, then having the secondary market adds some complexity but it doesn't really change the fundamental principle. If the mortgage looks bad, it's going to be harder to sell; it's going to be undesirable, it's going to be subprime. For a long time, both loan originators and secondary buyers avoided those loans because there was too much risk, too little information, and too much danger. Starting in the 1990s, because of changes in public policy and some fancy financial wizardry on Wall Street everything changed. A number of lenders started exempting borrowers from even the most minimal information demands. Inside the industry, they called these "liar loans" or "NINA loans" (NINA for "no income, no assets"). If you tell me you have enough money to pay the mortgage, I'll believe you. But why now, why would any rational lender accept a "blind date" with a NINA loan? That's just crazy. I can see why the originator of the loan doesn't care about the probability of performance, because it's selling the loan. Once it's sold the loan, the question is: Why would any of the buyers accept that heightened risk? I think they're persuaded by a blind date and a massive cascade that there really wasn't heightened risk, despite eliminating most of the protections. That would have been modern day alchemy if it had been true; but sadly, it was not.

Who was responsible for the changes? We have two players: Congress on the one hand and Wall Street on the other. First, the federal government became midwife to this large national, secondary mortgage market by creating institutions like the Federal National Mortgage Administration which all her friends call "Fannie Mae." Fannie Mae borrows money from the general public and then uses that to buy mortgages on the secondary market, ultimately financing mortgages all over the country. But the original lender over here has no information at all about the strength of the mortgage in the far end of that whole chain of events. They always relied on Fannie Mae to assess those; they always thought their risk was that Fannie Mae wouldn't be able to pay back, that Fannie Mae would default on the bonds. Surely Fannie Mae will do its own due diligence; Fannie Mae will take care that the mortgages are sound; and besides that, there's probably the full faith and credit o f the United States behind it.

In the 1990s, Congress started pushing Fannie Mae for policy change. It asked Fannie Male to lower its underwriting standards; it asked it that they push more funds toward low and very moderate income people who before had been priced out of the mortgage market. Who knew they were doing this? Certainly not all the people over here who were lending money to Fannie

Mae; they'd been taken on a blind date that they didn't even know they were on. On the other hand, there was the Wall Street financial engineering. Remember I said I was going to confuse you? Just bear with me; I'm going to see if I can't just make you crazy confused for the next couple minutes. As soon as you got home from your blind date with Fannie Mae, Wall Street was standing there with several other suitors waiting.

Wall Street figured out that it could make a profit if it would buy up whole packages, whole bundles, of these subprime mortgages, and use that whole portfolio as backing for something called a Mortgage Backed Security. Then it could get investors to buy Mortgage Backed Securities, which meant they were buying a share of the revenue from the portfolio of the subprime mortgages. These people were able to invest in high-yield subprime mortgages, and they didn't have to put all their eggs in one basket. It sounded good; they didn't need so much information on the individual loans because they were buying the sum total of them. Wall Street's profit, of course, was determined by how many of these securities they could sell; so there was this hunger on Wall Street: more and more subprime loans to feed this new market.

But the story goes on: We could then package Mortgage Backed Securities and use that package as collateral (the hostages) behind collateralized debt obligation. Then, in case there was any risk that the collateralized debt obligations wouldn't pay off, other companies like AIG started selling "insurance"—just follow me for a minute, this is going to be confusing—in the form of credit default swaps to pay off the collateralized debt obligations if the underlying Mortgage Backed Securities, based on portfolios of individual subprime mortgages, failed to perform; and on, and on. You've just been asked to go on a date with your cousin's best friend's brother's office mate's pen pal's teacher; how could anything possibly go wrong? By the time we had done all that, it was virtually impossible for the ultimate investors at the end of that chain to have any idea who actually and ultimately owed what to whom. You didn't know who you owed money to. You certainly couldn't assess accurately the likelihood of people repaying their loans. This whole structure created massive, massive uncertainty about risk.

But it really didn't matter, of course, because there was that final hostage that would guarantee repayment if this whole thing started to collapse. What was that? It was the value of the real estate itself. After all, housing prices always rise at least a little, don't they? Yes they do, until, like tulip bulbs, they don't. The underlying loans at the bottom of this whole obfuscated chain started to go bad; foreclosures rose; housing prices fell. More and more people found that they owed more on their mortgage than their house was currently worth; their mortgages had turned upside down. That creates an incentive to walk away. Once the hostage has died, its value as a deterrent is gone; and at that moment, in that panicked phase, suddenly everyone again became aware of their own level of ignorance. There was no reliable information to gauge the credit worthiness of anyone else. No one knew how much their own assets were worth, let alone the assets held by others. No collateral could really serve as a hostage. No one dared lend to anyone. Credit markets froze, consumers dared not buy, businesses dared not invest. The worst economic downturn in decades beset the world's economy.

If you look at that, if you see that through an economist's eyes, you can see that this whole crisis—the rise and the fall, the bubble and the burst—are really reflections of information asymmetry, rational ignorance, and risk. Far too many of us accepted a financial blind date, forgetting how easily trust can misplaced; not because everybody we deal with is inherently dishonest, but because, just like us, everyone we deal with faces inevitable uncertainty, ignorance, and risk. When we forget that is when we collectively get into some real trouble.

What do we take from all of this? First and foremost, we need to remember that our own inevitable uncertainty makes information itself strategic. Most of what we need to know we have to get from other people. Know when information asymmetry is going to make you vulnerable to a bad blind date. We face this time and again in handling our personal and national finances; and there the protection is a healthy dose of skepticism. Does your advisor's compensation create incentives that conflict with your objectives? If you're promised high, steady gains year after year with no significant risk, I think you should view an entreaty like that the way you do when you receive an email from that unknown Nigerian prince who keeps emailing me. You know, the one who keeps offering me a 10 percent commission if I'll just let him launder several million dollars through my bank account? I suppose it could be true; but I think it would be dangerous to stake too much on it.

In the next lecture, we're going to add to this the consideration of the famous fourth dimension in Einstein's characterization of the universe: We're going start talking about time; and economists are going to have a lot to say about that.

A Matter of Time—Predicting Future Values
Lecture 9

> Ben Franklin understood [the concept of compound interest]. At his death, he willed $500 to the city of Boston, but with a condition: He prohibited the city from drawing on that for 200 years; he wanted the power of compounding to work for 2 full centuries. When finally the city of Boston was able to get into that account and open it up, there was not $500 in there anymore: It was worth over $6.5 million.

Economic thinking is focused on how people will and should respond to their incentives, to the benefits and costs of their decisions. But a lot of those benefits and costs won't occur until sometime into the future. How does the timing affect the value of the incentives today? When we add time to the equation, it brings 2 new elements to rational decision making: the **real value of money** and the **time value of money**.

First, we look at the real value of money. Money is an abstract unit. We can use it to measure all kinds of important underlying things, but money is a highly elastic unit of

The actual value of money is based on its purchasing power.

measure. Inflation constantly changes the purchasing power of money and alters its real value. If we're going to make rational decisions, we need to look not at how many dollars are involved but at what the equivalent of those dollars is. What can they buy? This is the concept behind the **price index** the government uses to measure inflation. Not considering the effects of inflation on the value of money can lead to grievous mistakes.

But there's no perfect predictor of future inflation, so important decisions have to be made with incomplete information.

Second, we examine the time value of money, and of everything else. The question of timing matters not only because inflation changes the value of a dollar but also for a more subtle reason: People almost always prefer to have good things happen sooner and bad things happen later. Economists refer to this as pure time preference. If timing matters to you, then it is an important element in rational decision making. The time value of money is made up of 2 parts: **discounted present value** and **future value**. To give some precision to the concepts of present and future value, I'm going to offer you a choice. Do you want $1000 today or $1000 a year from today? Besides the fact that you simply want to have the money sooner, money you receive today can start to earn interest. If I have $1000 today and put it in an interest-bearing account at 5%, a year from now there will $1050 in it. Financially, $1000 today and $1050 in a year are equivalent events: $1050 is the 1-year future value of $1000 today. The concept of present value uses the same metaphorical balance scale, just starting from this side: If I'm going to have $1050 in a year, what's the present value I need to be equivalent? The answer is that $1000 today is the present value equivalent of $1050 a year from today.

> **Inflation constantly changes the purchasing power of money and alters its real value.**

The topic of future value naturally leads to the extraordinary topic of compounding. That $1000 turned into $1050 in a year; and in the second year, I'll be earning interest not just on the original $1000 but also on the $50 of first-year interest. As time goes on, with the magic of **compound interest**, I'll earn interest on interest as well as on the original principal. After 10 years, the $1000 will grow to more than $1600; after 30 years, more than $4300; and after 50 years, almost $12,000. As the interest accumulates, the original principal becomes less significant, because I'm mostly earning interest on past interest. The longer the time involved, the more spectacular the results. ■

compound interest: Interest earned based on the sum of the original principal plus interest accrued. Interest earned in one period is added to the principal for the next period. Over time, interest is increasingly being earned on interest from earlier periods. The result is exponential growth in total dollar value.

discounted present value: The current equivalent value of an event that will not occur until sometime in the future. The further away an event is, and the higher the discount rate, the lower its current, or discounted, present value.

future value: The dollar value at some point in the future of funds held today. Because of compounding interest, each dollar today will compound to more than a dollar in the future. The further into the future, the greater the future value.

nominal value: The value of anything expressed in dollars unadjusted for inflation. If the nominal price of something is $100, it is impossible to determine if that is high or low without knowing the purchasing power of a dollar.

price index: The proportionate cost of a given typical consumer market basket of goods relative to some arbitrary base year denoted as 100. A price index of 127 means that compared to the base year, it now takes 27% more dollars to buy the same bundle of goods.

real value of money: Money that has been adjusted to remove the effects of inflation or deflation. Using real money allows comparisons of actual value over time.

time value of money: The monetary value of an event or product adjusted for when it occurs or exists.

1. Time matters. *When* events, both good and bad, happen is an important element of evaluating options. Money is an elastic measure, and its real value changes as the cost of living changes. Any measure in dollar units must be examined to determine which type of dollars (nominal or real) are being used.

2. Because of interest, money also has a time value. The present equivalent of receiving $1000 at some point in the future becomes smaller and smaller as that event moves further into the future. Similarly, the longer interest accumulates on an amount of principal, the greater its compounded future value.

A Matter of Time—Predicting Future Values
Lecture 9—Transcript

Welcome back. This is going to be the ninth lecture in our series on "How to Think Like an Economist." We've really done a lot in the last few sessions: We developed an important toolkit of economic ideas that we can use; we've applied it in many different situations; we've talked about the importance of having well-defined rights and rules; we spent a lot of time talking about information and ignorance, and about uncertainty and about risk. But there's one more important topic we need to cover, and it's about time; literally. Today, we're going to think like economists about time itself.

I want to begin with a true story: In 1965, there was a 47-year-old French lawyer, and he entered into a contract with then-90-year-old Madame Jeanne Calment. She was a widow, she had no living heirs, and so he offered her $500 every month for the rest of her life if he she would give to him title to her Paris apartment when she died. In expected value terms, this looked like a pretty good deal for both of them. For her, she would be financially secure; she'd have a steady source of income. For him? He was likely to get a Paris apartment in the not too distant future, and likely at a real bargain price. However, defying all odds, and I guarantee you the expectations of both of them, Madame Calment lived to be 122; Monsieur Raffrey had died of cancer by then in his 70s. His widow was contractually obligated to continue the payments until 1977, when finally, Madame Calment and title to her apartment both passed on.

This tale is useful to us for two reasons: First, it gives us a chance to review the idea, the concepts, of "expected value" and the concepts of "risk" that we developed in the last lecture. Life expectancies are really good predictors of what's going to happen on average; but in individual cases, outcomes can be quite, quite different from the average. It was a rational decision for Monsieur Raffrey at the time he made it, but it's probably an important lesson to remember: Being rational doesn't protect you from uncertain and unfavorable future outcomes. When you maximize expected value, it doesn't guarantee that you're going to win every time, but it's the best bet you can make in an uncertain world. I expect that was small consolation to the poor lawyer. The second lesson that we're going to talk about is that this story introduces the important concept of rationality over time: When things happen matters a great deal. The wisdom of an agreement to trade a substantial amount of money for title to an apartment depends on the timing of those things. If they happen at the same moment, that's a very, very different transaction than if I pay you now and have to wait 32 years to take possession. Rational decision makers, like lawyers when they write contracts, should always include the clause "time is of the essence."

Economic thinking, as we know, is focused on how people will and should respond to their incentives, to the benefits and costs of their decisions. But an awful lot of the benefits and the costs that we face from decisions we make now don't occur until sometime into the future. How does the timing affect the value of the incentives today? We face decisions like that all the time. Should I pay cash for a new car, or should I finance it over 72 months? What's going to be the effect of waiting a few years if I begin building my retirement account? Personally, I keep hoping to have to face this decision: When I hold a winning $1 million lottery ticket, and it says on it in the fine print "Payable is $50,000 a year for 20 years," do I take it that way, or do I take it as a lump sum, all up front, even though it's going to be worth perhaps two-thirds that amount? How much is it going to take my children or grandchildren to get through four years of college in the future? How much saving is necessary today to ensure that they can? Our lives and the consequences of our choices are spread over time. If we're going to think rationally, if we're going to think like economists, we need to have our decisions reflect that.

How do economists think about choices when we have to decide today but the consequences will only occur at some point into the future? When we add time, it's going to bring two important new elements, two important decisions, to rational decision making. The first is we have to talk about the value of money itself; what's the real value? The second is we're going to have to talk how to value now, today, in the present, events that won't occur until sometime in the future, sometimes the distant future. We have two terms we're going to understand today: the real value of money and the time value of money; and we're going to consider each of those in turn.

Economics isn't really focused on money any more than physics is the science of kilograms; money and kilograms are abstract units. We can use them to measure all kinds of much more important underlying things; but money, the thing we use in financial decisions, is a really strange yardstick. Suppose we were planning to build a bridge, you and I, and I gave you a piece of elastic cord and I said, "I want you to use this as the measuring rod when you're constructing all the parts that are going to go on our bridge." I expect that when the final product was finally put together we'd find that those parts didn't work so well together. That would be nuts; use a piece of elastic as a measuring rod? Yet money, the yardstick that we do use to measure so many important elements, is really a very highly elastic unit of measure. Neither philosophically nor economically is money ever what life is all about, not even to an economist. If your primary goal was to acquire as much money as possible, perhaps you should have moved to Zimbabwe. In 2008, the legislature in Zimbabwe passed a minimum wage statute that raised the minimum wage in that country to $100 billion a month. That's more dollars than I'm going to make in my entire lifetime even if I, like Madame Calment, I live to be 122. You know there's a catch; what's the catch? The catch, of course, is $100 billion Zimbabwe, which, at the time, had a U.S. equivalence of about $13 U.S. The money in Zimbabwe literally wasn't worth the paper it was printed on.

I certainly hope that you and I never face that kind of hyperinflation; that's a disruption that throws all kinds of things into chaos. But it's a clear reminder that any time there's a change in price, any time there's inflation, it changes the underlying purchasing power of money and alters what we economists call its "real" value. Any time you say something and use a measure dollars, the first thing an economist is going to ask you: Which dollars are you using? Real dollars or nominal dollars? Dollars fixed in value, or dollars allowed to stretch or shrink as changes in price level take place. If we're really going to make rational decisions, then we need to think about the incentives, we need to think about the benefits, we need to think about the costs in the future in real terms, in fixed value dollar terms. It's never, ever a matter of how many dollars are involved; it's always a question of what's the equivalent of those dollars? What can the dollars buy? If my grandfather had retired with $1 million in a retirement account, he would have done very well indeed. If I do so, I'll probably get by comfortably. If my children do, it's possible they may barely be getting by. Any change in the value of a currency changes the consequences of our actions. We need to be conscious and aware of that at all times.

How do you measure inflation? How do you know how much inflation there is? Fortunately the government is probably going to do that for you, and they measure inflation using something called a "price index," and the most commonly used of that is something called the "Consumer Price Index." Here's how it's constructed: They take a conceptual market basket of goods and say that's what a typical household is going to buy; that's what it needs to live for a year. Then it picks a base year, it doesn't matter what year—let's say 1995—and it says: How many dollars would it take to buy that basket of goods in 1995? They set the cost of living in that base year: 1995 = 100. If we come back in 2005 and it takes 50 percent more dollars to buy the same stuff, the price index for 2005 is going to be 150. Each dollar buys two-thirds of what it did; it takes 50 percent more dollars to buy the same stuff. A 2005 dollar is the equivalent of $.67 in terms of 1995 dollars. You can, and in some situations clearly should, take the time to convert nominal dollars to real dollars; so let's compare them, let's see what the consequence is over time.

How about an example? I like to call this one "My In-laws' Big Investment." My in-laws raised, educated, and sent through college five children and a couple of cousins, and after they'd done all that they had very little money to put into a retirement fund until late in life; and mostly they retired on the value that they'd accumulated in their beautiful old house. They bought a lovely house in central Phoenix, Arizona in 1955 and I think they paid something like $20,000 for it. When they finally moved out in 2001, they sold the exact same house for $400,000. They took out 20 times more dollars than they put in. That seems incredibly profitable; but what's the question they need to ask? Are those nominal dollars, or are those real dollars? A 2001 dollar was worth only about what $.15 was worth in 1955. They did take out 20 times more dollars, but each dollar was worth about one-sixth of the dollars in its starting value. They had a real return, they made a profit off it; the increase in value was about 3 times, though, not 20 times. That's ok, but it's nowhere near as spectacular as it first appeared. Not to consider the effects of inflation on the value of money can lead us to make grievous mistakes. At even a modest inflation rate, three percent a year, a dollar is going to lose a quarter of its value in 10 years. In the 1980s, when we had double digit inflation in the United States, we were experiencing the dollar losing about three-quarters of its value over a decade. You need to know real or nominal value.

It's one thing to know that you should anticipate inflation; it's another to figure out what the rate is likely to be. Wouldn't it be nice if you had a crystal ball? What is the inflation rate going to be in the future? The answer to that question is the same as it is to all complex questions: it depends, and it depends on lots of things. Important decisions, however, are going to have to be made with incomplete information; there's no perfect predictor of future inflation. But wait a minute; we talked earlier in one of these lectures about the wisdom of the crowd; remember back in Lecture 6? Where James Surowieki had this book and he said if we can somehow find a way to get an estimator where we take all the diverse knowledge and pack it together, independent predictions or estimates, they might converge on the "correct" answer. No one expert could tell us where the lost submarine was going to be, but the average of the experts' estimates brought us awfully close.

Is there anything equivalent to this? Anything like the Iowa Electronic Markets that we talked about before; a place where all the information from all the disparate players in the game gets aggregated and averaged? Many economists think there is. After the very dismal experience in the United States in the 1970s and 80s with inflation, in the 1990s the federal government decided to create a new kind of financial asset. They called them "Treasury Inflation Protected Securities" or "TIPS" for short. They're just like regular U.S. bonds; the default risk is absolutely minimal; they enjoy the full faith and credit of the United States; but unlike regular bonds, the principle when it's returned is going to get adjusted using the Consumer Price Index. The nominal return, the percentage, depends on changes in the value of the dollar, but the real return is going to be guaranteed.

Here's what happens: The government auctions off regular bonds, and it auctions off TIPS bonds, and the difference between those two is the crowd's best estimate of future inflation; all of the players in the financial game. If 10 year unprotected bonds are returning five percent, and 10 year TIPS bonds are two percent, what's the market's best estimate of future inflation? About three percent a year; 5 – 2. Even if you don't know and don't buy government bonds, it's probably a good thing to know what inflation's likely to be because it affects so many of the decisions that you make. Remember, that three percent isn't a guarantee; it's only the best collective estimate. As Monsieur Raffrey found out, sometimes even the very best estimates can turn out to be off by quite a lot.

The second thing we need to talk about is the time value of money, and of everything else. "When" matters not only because inflation changes the value of a dollar, there's a more subtle reason as well. Let me see if I can try this on you: I'm going to offer you a Caribbean vacation today, or the same vacation in 5 years. Which would you prefer? It's the same trip, why does it matter when? Or alternatively, how about a root canal this afternoon or in 10 years? It's the same procedure; why would you care when? Apparently, though, you cared; and psychologists tell us that most people care. We don't really have reasons why, but the evidence is strong: Humans almost always prefer to have good things happen sooner and bad things happen later. Economists call that "pure time preference"; and if "when" matters to you, then "when" is an important element in rational decision making. If the value of the incentives guiding your choices is going to be affected by "when," we need to know how events now compare to events later. For economists, who seem to have ways of attaching dollar values to everything, the answer lies in what we call the "time value of money" and its two constituent parts: "present value" and "future value." Let's talk about present value; valuing the future today.

If you stand on the shore and watch a ship sail toward the horizon, to your eye it's getting smaller and smaller and smaller the farther away it is. Objectively, you know it's always the same size; it's the perspective that changes. From the shore, the ship seems to be shrinking. The time value of money in both economic and financial terms is pretty much like that. To receive $1,000 is to receive $1,000; but the date at which that happens matters, and when the time you receive the money gets farther and farther into the future, just like a ship on the horizon, it appears to us standing here that in the present, its value is shrinking.

Here's a simple example: To perhaps give some precision to our concepts of present and future value, I'm going to offer you a choice. Do you want $1,000 today or $1,000 a year from today; which? Both financially and psychologically, those are not equivalent events; "when" matters. Besides simply liking it to happen sooner, money today can earn interest. If I have the $1,000 today and I put it in an interest-bearing account at five percent, when I open that up a year from now there will be more than $1,000 in it; at five percent, there will be $1,050 in it. Financially, those are the two options that are equivalent events: $1,000, $1,050 in a year; if I put those on a metaphorical balance scale, they just match. $1,050 is the one year future value, the future equivalent, of having $1,000 today. The concept of "present value" uses the same metaphorical balance scale, it's just starting from this side; it's looking from the perspective of the ship rather than the shore. If I'm going to have $1,050 in a year, what do I need to have now to get there? What's the present value I need to be equivalent? The answer is $1,000 today is the present value equivalent of $1,050 a year from today. That's going to affect our economic thinking.

Let's go back to my unfortunately unrealized fantasy: The day I'm going to have that $1 million lottery ticket where it says, "Payable as $50,000 a year for 20 years." If you add that up, 20 payments of $50,000 adds up to $1 million; but that's not the same thing as getting $1 million today. If you think about it for a minute, they're very, very different. If I had the $1 million today and I put it in the bank and I could earn five percent that would throw off $50,000 each year not for 20 years, for eternity; and at every moment I would also still have a full $1 million in the bank. Those are not equivalent events; they do not have the same value. When things happen matters. If you do all the fancy math—and I'm not going to do it today—$50,000 a year for 20 years at five percent, the present value of that stream is about $623,000. If you started with that in the bank and you took out $50,000 a year, using up the interest, eating into the principle, the account would slowly fall down and hit zero when? Right at the end of year 20. $623,110 today and $50,000 a year for 20 years are the equivalent events; the lump sum at the front is what we call the "discounted present value" of that stream of payments.

An annuity, of course, is kind of a mirror image of winning the lottery. Instead of receiving a lump sum, you pay a bunch up front and you buy a stream of payments into the future. In essence, that's what Madame Calment did; remember: She traded the title to her apartment for a lifetime stream of payments. That worked out pretty well for her; unfortunately, you can't always count on beating the actuarial odds the way she did.

I want to add another wrinkle to this: Once we've started talking about future value and the way in which money can grow over time, the time value of money, I want to talk a little bit about the magic of compounding; it's extraordinary. When each of our three children graduated from high school, their mother and I gave them $1 million (potential, because we're not that rich). But if it fulfills that potential, it won't be because we were generous; it will be because of the timing and the conditions of our gift, and our children coming to understand the magical power of compounding. Here's how it worked: What we really gave them was a mutual fund worth about $3,000 each when they turned 18; and then their mom and I said, "We'll add $100 each month to that account until the day you withdraw the first penny. Take out a dime, we're done." Even if we're compelled to stop when we reach retirement age, if they leave it there until they reach their retirement age, $1 million in that account is not out of the question. How does so little become so much? The answer is "time."

Remember the choice I offered a few minutes ago; $1,000 now or $1,000 in a year? That $1,000 now at 5 percent turned into $1,050 in a year; and in the second year, I'd be earning interest not just on the original $1,000, but on the $50 of first-year interest. As time goes on, with the magic of compounding, you're earning interest on interest on interest plus, of course, the original principal. After 10 years, the $1,000 at 5 percent would have grown to almost $1,600; after 30 years it would have grown to more than $4,300; after 50 years, it would have grown to almost $12,000. As the interest accumulates, the original principle becomes less and less important, it becomes less significant, because mostly we're earning interest on past interest. The better the return, the more spectacular the results. At a 10 percent rate of return— which is in the neighborhood of what the stock market has returned in nominal terms over a long period of time—$1,000 in 30 years would become $17,000; and after 50 years $117,000. $3,000 plus that monthly $100 add-in their mom and I promised, by the time our kids age 65, if those conditions all hold there will be more than $1 million in each of their accounts. The longer the time involved, the more spectacular the results.

Ben Franklin understood that. At his death, he willed $500 to the City of Boston, but with a condition: He prohibited the city from drawing on that for 200 years; he wanted the power of compounding to work for two full centuries. When finally the City of Boston was able to get into that account and open it up, there was not $500 in there anymore, it was worth over $6.5 million. I don't think I can reasonably ask my kids to wait quite that long to use their gift; but if they're patient, as we've asked them to be, they're going to do very well with it.

That's a lesson that's probably best learned young. In recent years, Smith College, where I teach, has instituted a number of noncredit courses on basic financial literacy before we cast the students out into the "real" world. When we began a few years ago, we got lots of national press on this. The *Today* show from NBC sent a crew so that they could show a piece on their morning TV broadcast; and they happened to come the day I was talking about the importance of giving compounding time to work on your savings. The 20-year-old students seemed to be sitting there with a "hmmm, that's kind of interesting" attitude; but when I looked at the camera crew, most of whom seemed to be in their late 40s, there were tears trickling down their cheeks. After we were done, they lamented to me, "Why didn't anyone tell me this when I was their age?"

The real graduation gift to our children isn't the money—though I'm sure they're going to appreciate that—it was an opportunity to understand at a young age the power of compounding, and how that depends on time; and that the future value literally grows exponentially. The longer compounding has to work, the more spectacular the result. Time is of the essence for economists, as well as for contract lawyers; and time is of the essence for you as well when you're making rational decisions. When thinking about decisions, always consider the economic consequences of "when." Teach your children, or your grandchildren, to think like that as well. Make sure they know that the time to assure a comfortable retirement is in your youth. Your 50s is not the time to start planning for retirement, something almost of us discover when we reach our 50s. It's my hope that our "million dollar gift" to our children is going to make it clear to them.

I want to end with a fun story, and it kind of captures some of the concepts we've been talking about today. As the year 2000 was approaching on the horizon, *The Economist* magazine published a fantasy tale. They imagined a young girl born in 1900, and they gave her a name; they called her Felicity Foresight. They endowed her with two things: $1, and perfect information about the future. On December 31 of each year, she would move all her accumulated wealth into the asset class that was poised on the brink of doing the absolute best in the coming year—one year it would be U.S. stocks, another European bonds, a third gold futures, etc.—and they let that magic work for a full century. Their hypothetical young woman grew to maturity and even old age, and they let that wealth compound year after year until she reached her 100th birthday. As the new millennium dawned, they calculated that her $1 birthday gift would have grown to be greater than $9.6 quintillion. Let me say that again: $9.6 quintillion. The compounded rate of return was about 55 percent. I expect a large share of it probably would have gone for lawyers' fees because they didn't include taxes when they were doing the calculations, and she seems to have dodged paying brokerage fees; but even if we had included those, her performance would have been nothing short of remarkable.

We can use her story to try out our new economist's vocabulary. When we put her performance on our metaphorical balance scale, what's the present value today of $9.6 quintillion 100 years into the future? Using a discount rate of 55 percent, it's just $1. What's the future value of $1 today if we could invest it with an annual return of 55 percent? Why it would only be $9.6 quintillion. That leaves us with two pressing questions: First, suppose Madame Calment had at 100 as much as Felicity did; in the mere 22 years she had left to spend it, could she have spent it all? The answer, of course, is absolutely not; on that amount of money, the interest alone would be several trillion dollars a day. Second, and probably more subtle, what's the first thing an economist says when he hears that story? "Are you talking nominal or real dollars?" After all, $9.6 quintillion doesn't buy what it used to.

What should you take away from this lecture? First, we always need to distinguish between nominal and real measures of costs and benefits of our actions. It's never a matter of just how many dollars are involved, but also the purchasing power of each dollar when prices change over time; we have to consider that, we have to be aware of that. How can you measure that? The best way is using price indices such as the Consumer Price Index, which measures year-to-year changes in the purchasing power of the dollar. How can we predict future inflation, and as a result future declines in purchasing power? One possibility is the spread between regular U.S. Treasury Bonds and special Treasure Inflation Protected Securities, the TIPS bonds. Second, we always need to recognize that moving an event into the future reduces its equivalent present value. As interest rates rise, the difference between the present and future values of events grows. "When" does matter.

We've covered quite a lot. In the next lecture, what I'd like to do is to take several of these large themes that we've talked about and see if we can draw them together into a couple of examples, where we can practice our economic thinking skills. We'll use all these multiple elements, and we'll see if we can encounter them in a surprisingly complex decision or two when we go shopping. It's probably the first time you've ever taken your thinking like an economist skills to the mall. I think you're going to be surprised at just how much fun that can actually be.

Think Again—Evaluating Risk in Purchasing
Lecture 10

> For many of us, risk has its own cost; or for some of us, its own reward. Recall when we've talked about people we've always measured their welfare—it's their own self-evaluated quality of life. It's never about money per se; it's never about material goods. Rationality meant choosing whatever alternative improves your self-defined quality of life. For you to go on a rafting trip just because you won a ticket would be irrational if you have an intense fear of drowning, no matter what the market value of the trip. To turn down that trip would be irrational if you have an intense love of adventure travel.

Let's examine a recent purchase that I made and use some of the concepts developed in this course to determine whether I made a rational decision. I was buying a new television, and the sales associate tried to persuade me to purchase the extended warranty contract. The economist's tool kit gave me a framework to think about this problem. The decision involved risk, **uncertainty**, and information asymmetry.

The sales associate tried to help me overcome my rational ignorance. He freely offered me lots of information on repair risks, but I knew that I couldn't trust that information to be unbiased. I don't think he was lying; I just think he was using information selectively to influence my assessment of the risks that I faced. What I really wanted was unbiased information on the true expected value of repairs using real objective probabilities, but where could I get that at a reasonable cost? I suppose I could have asked him to wait while I went to the library and invested several days doing online research on the likelihood of that television needing repairs over time. But that would have been impractical, so instead I applied shortcuts that we've learned about thinking like an economist.

First, I applied the 6 foundation principles and 3 core concepts. Remember that people, including those who own giant electronics chains, respond to incentives. So if those owners are strategic and rational, and have all the information I need, is there a way I can get them to reveal it to me? Of course—they already have. Here's how: I know that a company will price the warranties so that they will make a substantial profit on them. They don't share with me the underlying data or calculations, but their enthusiasm for selling me that contract gave me confidence that they were asking a price well above the discounted present value of the expected value of the repairs. But how could I tell if their offered contract price was too much above the cost, if it was unreasonable? Sometimes even the simplest of comparisons based on your own experience or that of your friends is enough for you to gauge the reasonableness of a contract. They were asking me to pay 15% of the purchase price for protection in years 2 and 3, after the manufacturer's warranty ran out. I thought about my anecdotal knowledge of televisions, and the probability that the television would self-destruct in year 2 or 3 seemed low. But a ballpark estimate told me that there would have to be about a 1 in 7 chance of that happening for me to rationally pay for their extended warranty. It was pretty obvious that there was a substantial overestimate of the real probabilistic risk in the contract price.

The economist's tool kit helps us navigate complex decisions.

What about the factor of time? Remember, they were asking me to pay a premium today for protection that would begin in the future. If I'm paying it all up front, before I'm even covered, that raises the real cost of the contract. Another troubling factor was the lack of competition: They were offering me the extended warranty in a context that had no competition and no alternatives. I was pretty confident that the price of the contract they were offering was quite a bit above the expected value of any future repairs. Clearly it was going to be a good deal for them but not such a good deal for me.

Buying that contract would have been irrational: The cost almost certainly exceeded any value of the benefits.

All I needed to reach that conclusion was the framework of thinking like an economist. But what if I had nagging doubts? What if I thought I was the one outlier whose television would inexplicably explode the day the factory warranty expired? Won't I regret not having bought the warranty? Actually, if I think like an economist about all the purchases I make, then I won't. If I took all the money that I would have spent for contracts on all my major purchases and put it in a reserve account earning a little interest, I guarantee you the funds in that account would be enough to cover all future repairs. Buying that contract would have been irrational: The cost almost certainly exceeded any value of the benefits.

There's one last piece to this puzzle. If I am **risk averse**—if I am the kind of person who will lie awake every night trembling with fear that someday I may have to pay a large television repair bill—then I should be willing to pay for a warranty. In this case, I'm not paying to protect the television but rather to protect myself from the discomfort of risk. Even though the price of the protection is greater than the present value of the expected value of the repairs, it can make me better off. Thinking like an economist gives me a framework to shape my decisions. ∎

risk aversion: A preference for a certain option over a risky option with an identical expected value. Risk aversion stems from psychological discomfort arising from the mere existence of risk.

uncertainty: Any situation in which there is less than perfect information. Increases and improvements in information reduce uncertainty.

Take-Away Points

1. A seemingly simple decision (e.g., forgoing an offer for an extended warranty contract) in fact is a complex conjunction of many important aspects of thinking like an economist. To decide rationally is to understand what that contract consists of and to be able to evaluate rationally its reasonableness.

2. Even when the hard data is missing for a complete calculation of a complex number—like the discounted present value of a stream of expected values for repairs—thinking like an economist provides us with both a framework for analyzing choices and shortcuts for estimating the boundaries of reasonableness.

Think Again—Evaluating Risk in Purchasing
Lecture 10—Transcript

Hello once again. Welcome back for Lecture 10 in our series on "How to Think Like an Economist." I want to do a couple of somewhat different things today. The first thing I want to do is I want to take you shopping with me. I want to take a look at a single purchase that my wife and I recently made and see whether we can use some of the concepts we've developed to determine whether or not what we decided was in truth the rational decision. In the process of that, I want to look at a couple of shortcuts that you can use to take some of these really somewhat sophisticated concepts and make them practical and useable in everyday experience. Finally, we're going to venture a little more distantly and differently into the behavioral economics field, and we're going to explore a little bit some of how feelings about risk can and should affect our choices.

Let me start with a confession: When it comes to new technology, my wife and I are never what you'd call early adopters. I have no idea how many years we sat and watched a bulky, old, square-screened TV set; it had a giant picture tube and weighed about 200 pounds. But eventually technological change is going to come to even those who resist it as much as we did. One day not too long ago, our ancient television finally died, and we were forced into the complex world of flat screen television. We packed up and we went to one of the giant electronics stores, and were confronted with dozens of options. Liquid crystal, plasma, rear projection; they kept quoting initials I have no idea what they mean: dpi, HD, more and more. We finally picked out one based on the very sophisticated criteria in that, "Hey, that picture looks pretty good to us." It wasn't one of those monster TVs, but it's a big step up from what we've been looking at for years.

As he was writing up the sale, our sales associate—who I swear could not have been more than 19 years old—stated to us as an obvious fact, it wasn't a question it was a fact: "And, of course, you will want the extended warranty contract, won't you sir?" "No thanks," I said, "I think we're going to skip that." He looked at me like that was the most irresponsible and incomprehensible answer he'd ever heard. "Wait," he said, "before you decide that you should definitely speak to my manager." Clearly there was a script here; there was a process to be followed when anyone was audacious enough to turn down the extended warranty. The manager shows up, he looked at me with an incredulous stare in his eyes, and I repeated to him our decision that we didn't think we'd buy the extended warranty. He raised one eyebrow and in seeming shock he said to me, "May I ask why not, sir?" He had a ready response prepared, I think, to any possible objection anyone could raise; but he was not ready for me.

"This," I said, "is a teachable moment." Virtually everything that we've covered in this course was relevant to his one simple question, and I was not going to pass up the opportunity to help this young man learn to think like an economist. "Of course you may ask why not," I replied. "First, I guesstimated the possible repairs that might be needed over the life of the television and the costs associated with each so that I could form expected value calculations on repairs. Then, based on rationally imperfect information, I formed subjective probability estimates about those repairs. Then I had a stream of expected values for repair costs distributed over the life of the television. But some, of course, would not occur until far in the future; so I had to decide which repairs would occur when. Finally," I told him, "I used current interest rates, and I used that to discount the entire stream of future expected values backward to get a single discounted present value for the contract protection. When I compared that number to the price you asked for the contract, the rational choice, obviously, is to decline the extended warranty." I smiled politely.

He stared at me with an expression on his face that I have never seen before or since. He clearly was scanning his memorized script, trying to find the appropriate response to that answer, and he came up blank. Finally he just mumbled "Okay" and walked away. There are very few moments in life when it's just plain fun to be an economist; and when they come along like that, you have to savor them to the absolute fullest.

I have to be honest with you and confess that I really wasn't being completely honest with him. I was describing how I thought about his offer, but I obviously didn't have enough data, I didn't have enough time, and I certainly didn't have the raw mathematical skill in my head to do all of that calculation right then and there. But this economist's toolkit we've developed, this way of thinking, game me a framework to think about this problem, and I knew this was a decision involving many of our concepts. First, it clearly involved risk; we're talking about uncontrollable probabilistic events. It involved uncertainty; I clearly had incomplete information and would have to make the decision without information. It was clearly a case of extreme what Akerloff called "information asymmetry." The company knew what I needed to know if I was going to make a wise choice, but I didn't know it. I also knew that there was a blind date waiting; that they were going to use the asymmetry as best they could to their strategic advantage. That was how I thought about the decision; what I lacked was enough information to do the kind of precise calculations I'd told him I'd done.

Of course, my sales associate was trying to help me overcome my rational ignorance; he freely offered me lots of information on repair risks; I thought it must be a little bit selective. "You know," he said, "that if the main 'whatzit' goes out, that could cost several hundred dollars, not counting labor. But if you have the warranty, it'll cost you nothing. You know you'll be glad you have the protection. You can't really put a price on peace of mind." I'd been on enough blind dates to know that you can't trust all that free information to be unbiased or reliable. I don't think he was lying, I just think he was using the information selectively because he knew I had to make a subjective assessment of the risks that I faced. What I really wanted was unbiased information on the true expected value of repairs using the real objective probabilities, but where could I get that at a reasonable cost? I needed some shortcuts, and thinking like an economist provided me with a couple of them. One thing I could have done, I suppose, was say, "Wait, hold everything; stay here. I'm going to go to the library for a while; I'm going to get on the internet; I'm going to invest several days doing original research to try and figure out what is the likelihood of repairs of a television of that model spread over time. But that would be impractical and expensive in opportunity cost if not in dollars. Is there a faster way to get a handle on that?

I think there is if you apply the Foundation Principles and the Core Concepts. Remember, economists think that people, including those who own and manage giant electronics chains, respond to incentives; and if those managers are strategic and rational, and they already have all the information I need, is there any way I can get them to reveal it to me? Of course, from thinking about this like an economist, I realized they just had. Here's how: I know that a company like that has very talented and sophisticated finance people at the home office, and they're told that their job is to price the contracts so that they will make a substantial profit on them; and I'm positive that those finance people know how to calculate expected values, they know how to calculate present values, I know that they had all the raw data necessary to do that, and I was confident that they'd calculated both of them. They were under instructions to price it at a comfortable profit margin. They didn't share with me the underlying data, they didn't share with me the calculations; but their clear enthusiasm for trying to get me to buy that contract at the offer price gave me confidence that they were asking a price well above the discounted present value of the expected value of the repairs. That's what a warranty is all about.

But was it so much above their cost that it made little sense for me to buy it? After all, the price of the television is greater than the costs of production; businesses need to make profits if they're going to survive. How could I tell if their offered contract price was too much above the cost? How could I tell if it was unreasonable? I needed information on the expected value of repairs. Sometimes even the simplest of comparisons based on your own experience or your friends, done in your head, is enough for you to gauge the reasonableness of a contract like that. I once bought a snow blower from one of the largest retailers in the country; I think I paid about $1,000. When it came, there was a standard warranty for the first 12 months; anything that went wrong, they would cover. As we reached the end of that period, I got a phone call; and the person on the other end was offering me—you guessed it—an extended warranty on any necessary repairs for three more years. She said, "You'll surely want to protect your investment in that fine machine. You wouldn't want to risk having the shock of a major repair bill, would you?" I said, "What does it cost?" She said, "Well, I can extend your warranty today for only $350 a year."

You don't need a lot of math skill and you don't need a lot of experience to evaluate that offer, do you? If we're talking about expected value, over three years the cost of the premiums on that contract would have been more than the machine itself cost. That would only make sense if the probability of total failure was more than one in three each of those years. That was crazy.

Either they sold me an incredibly defective machine or that was a terribly overpriced contract; and if the machine was that bad, I wish they would have told me about it before they sold it to me. I ultimately had more faith in the quality of the machine than they did, so I passed; but luckily for the poor young woman on the other end of that phone call, she didn't make the mistake of asking me why.

If we go back to the question of the television and its extended warranty, the contract price they were asking for years two and three wasn't that high, but it was still about 15 percent of the purchase price; not one third as it had been for the snow blower. But again, think if you will about your own experiences with televisions, your friends' experiences with televisions; a ballpark estimate that there would have to be at that price about a one in seven chance that the television would self-destruct sometime in years two and three. It could happen; but my experience with televisions, my friends who complain greatly if anything goes bad in their lives, made that seem unrealistically high. It was pretty obvious to me that there was a substantial overestimate of the real probabilistic risk in the contract price.

What about time, the topic we covered in the last lecture? "When" always matters. How is that relevant here? Remember, they were asking me to pay a premium today; for protection, it would begin two or three years into the future. The premium for the insurance is a present value for an event that doesn't occur until the future. If I'm paying it all up front, months before I'm even covered—that's what they were asking me to do—that just makes it that much more expensive. Now what do I have? I have two of these "back of the envelope" shortcuts that I can use to evaluate a purchase like this. The first is my own experience with products and reasonable, ballpark estimates that there's going to be a likelihood of major repairs. I also know that their asking me to pay it all up front for protection that doesn't even begin until years in the future is raising the real cost of the contract. Money has time value; they didn't seem to think that mattered.

There's another aspect of this that's always crucial for an economist. Economists like competition; and the extended warranty that they were offering me was offered in a context that had no competition and no alternatives. Whenever economists think broadly about economic performance or when economists are buying things, they really like competition. When they're selling, they are just like everyone else and hate it; but when they're buying, they think it's important. Whenever there's a product that the price is substantially above the actual cost, there's a strong incentive for other people to come in, sell below that price, take away the business, and still make a profit. The presence of competition is always protection for buyers. When we walked into that store looking to buy a television set, we know that there was a lot of competition for the sale of televisions. In our Sunday paper there are dozens of inserts that list the prices that all the retailers are going to charge; they're all promising to match any competitor's price; I know that there are free websites where I can compare the prices of the television at a number of competitors. When we walked into that store we were protected, we were armed with clear knowledge that we had lots of options for buying TVs. We knew what the market felt was a fair price; we knew that if they tried a hard sell on that TV, if they offered a price out of line, we could with confidence walk out the door. Knowledge of, and access to, ready alternatives is power and protection.

But once that TV sale was negotiated, the contract was a different kind of transaction. This was a one-time-only opportunity to buy, a single seller, fixed price, take it now or never. I already knew from the analytic shortcuts we talked about that the contract price was probably quite above the expected value of the repairs; and I also knew from my economic training that without the discipline of competition it was probably quite highly above. I'd been in situations like this before. When my daughter graduated from college, she could no longer be covered on our family's health insurance, the one that's paid by my employer (or at least partly paid by my employer). She needed alternate coverage, but she was young, she was healthy; probably she wouldn't have any need for expensive medical care. Probably. But a medical crisis with no insurance can be financially devastating for years to come, and we dared not leave her uncovered. The probability was small, the expected value was low, but if that worst case scenario had played out, that would have been very bad indeed.

We were offered a very easy option: We got a form from the insurance company that carries the employment policy, and they said, "You can continue that if you'd like, you just have to pick up the full cost. All it would require is check here, a simple notice, and her coverage can continue just as it has before." They also quoted the price, and the employer part plus the individual part that would now both belong to us had a quoted price of about $5,000 per year for coverage. It was a good policy, it had broad coverage, had minimal copays, virtually no deductible; but if they had said, "You must check this now or the offer will go away forever," I don't know what I would have done. With no better alternative, we probably would have ended up purchasing that policy. But the premiums seemed awfully high for a healthy 22 year old. It seemed at first like we had no choice, but fortunately we didn't have to check the box at that minute; we had an option to go look for other alternatives. It took a bit of research; we found that there were options. In fact, in the state where she was living, it was possible to buy a kind of limited individual policy that had a high $2,500 deductible each year and the premium was about $1,500 a year.

At first glance, you think about that, you say, "That sounds a little crazy." Because in a normal year, she'll pay $1,500 in health insurance and she'll receive absolutely no dollar benefits from that policy; because it's pretty unlikely that a 22 year old is going to incur more than $2,500 in medical costs. She's covered for catastrophic events; but all her regular care is coming out of her pocket. Is that nuts? Buy health insurance that doesn't help pay your health costs? But think about the worst case scenario for a moment: Even if she had to pay the full deductible plus the whole premium, the maximum she'd have to pay is $4,000. It wasn't covered from dollar one, but that was better in financial terms than the "gold plate" policy. The competing policy guaranteed an annual expense of $1,500 on the bottom and $4,000 on the top; and no matter how we ran the numbers, that $5,000 policy, while it was good insurance, was just irrationally expensive. But you know we only could find that out because we had the time, we could take the effort, to seek alternatives, to find alternate ways to do it, and that's how we found out that the price was way beyond what was reasonable to expect. Open competition is what made it easier for us to figure out whether the price was too high.

Let's go back to that TV service contract for a moment. Remember how that's structured: You've bought the TV, and now the pressure is buy, right now, one time only, before you leave this store, now or never offer. Their reluctance to allow me an opportunity to compare alternatives to an economist's mind was an indication that they already knew that their price was unreasonably high. That was probably wise on their part. A study in the *New York Times* said that third party maintenance contracts, when you can find them, typically sell for less than half the cost of those in the store/right now/gotta buy it/ time of purchase service contracts. Despite not having enough information to do all the hard calculations I tried to tell the manager I'd done, thinking like an economist had raised three red flags. The first was, from my own experience, experience alone, I know that the implied expected value of needing that full replacement coverage in years two and three seemed unrealistically high; I don't think that was an accurate estimate of the risk. Second, the request that they pay now for coverage we won't even see for two years did not, to me, seem to recognize the important time value of money. It didn't recognize that "when" matters, but as an economist I know that it always does. Finally, the structure of the offer that made it impossible for us to do comparison shopping, to look at other alternatives, was an indication again to me the seller knew that the offered terms would not compare favorably, and they were trying to prevent me from having that opportunity.

When all was said and done after all this, I was pretty confident that the price of the contract they were offering was quite a bit above the expected value of any future repairs. Clearly it was going to be a good deal for them, but it wasn't clearly such a good deal for me; and all I needed to reach that conclusion was the framework of thinking like an economist; I didn't really need all the hard data, I didn't really need all of the careful measures. Just the framework was enough to reach that conclusion. As had been with my daughter's health insurance, it really made more sense for us to risk incurring some repair costs than to pay a certain cost for repair insurance that was unreasonably expensive.

What if there's that nagging doubt? What if you think you were the truly unlucky buyer, the one outlier, the one whose TV inexplicably explodes to a certain death the day the factory warranty expires? At that moment, won't you regret not having bought the insurance? Probably momentarily you will, but if you think like an economist in this way about all the purchases you make, then the answer even then is likely to be no; because if you apply this thinking to all the multiple products that you're faced with every year that come with extended warranty offers—televisions, CD players, DVD players, refrigerators, cars, computers and all their peripherals—if you take the money that you would have spent for all those contracts, you put it in a reserve account to earn a little interest, unless you are the unluckiest person ever to walk the face of the earth, I'm going to tell you that the funds in that account will be enough to cover all the future repairs, and there will be something left over to help with your retirement party. Trust me; at least in clear mathematical terms, buying that contract would have been irrational. The cost almost certainly exceeded any value of the benefits. Story over; conclusion reached. That was the rational decision.

Yet we do buy contracts like this all the time; people do it every day. Are they all mistaken? Did they fail to understand what's involved? Worse yet, are they being irrational? In truth, we're not really like Mr. Spock; we're not hard wired to make all our decisions on the basis of immutable logic. We are, after all, humans who make our decisions in kind of a rich context of emotion. I want to talk for a moment about the cost, the un-comfort of risk itself, and this is going to take us toward the area of behavioral economics.

For many of us, risk has its own cost; or for some of us, its own reward. Recall when we've talked about people we've always measured their welfare; it's their own self-evaluated quality of life. It's never about money per se, it's never about material goods; rationality meant choosing whatever alternative improves your self-defined quality of life. For you to go on a rafting trip just because you won a ticket would be irrational if you have an intense fear of drowning, no matter what the market value of the trip. To turn down that trip would be irrational if you have an intense love of adventure travel. Economic thinking never tells you how you should feel about rafting trips, the opera, or ice fishing. It cannot tell you how you should feel about risk. Clearly, though, people do have strong feelings about risk itself, and different people do value it differently. Some of us fear risk, some are neutral towards it, and there's some who seek it out. To behave rationally in the economist's sense is to respond to one's own feelings about risk. Let me see if I can give some content to that particular concept.

I'm going to ask you to choose between two mutually exclusive options. First, you can have a 50 percent chance of winning $150 and a 50 percent chance of winning $50. The expected value of that if you'll think back to our earlier lecture would be an expected value of $100. You can have that, or I'll just give you $100 up front. The expected values of those two events are equal, but not many people see them as equal alternatives. There are some people for whom risk itself is a cost; it makes them uncomfortable, it makes them nervous, they dislike it, and we call those people "risk averse." They will always choose the $100 option, and in order to get them to choose the risky option we'd have to make its expected value much higher ($110, $115). They must be compensated for the discomfort, the cost of bearing risk itself; they don't like it. For others, there's some positive value in risk; they sort of like the gamble. After all, skydiving is not just a way to save time when deplaning; the risk itself is part of the appeal. The small prospect of a big score makes participating enticing. Lots of people, even if they know the expective value of a lottery ticket is $.06 will buy it anyway, because just the rush associated with the possibility that there might be a $50,000 payoff makes it worthwhile. Without risk seekers, state lotteries would soon go broke. Finally, there are some people who are risk neutral; and as far as they're concerned, those two options I gave you are equal because the expected values are equal. But I think they're in a distinct minority. Most of us clearly dislike, or occasionally enjoy, risk; it matters to us.

There's one last piece to this protection against future possible future losses puzzle. If you're risk averse, if you're the kind of person who won't enjoy that new TV, if you're going to lie awake every night trembling with fear that someday in the future it may require a large repair bill, you aren't going to enjoy your new TV; and you probably should be willing to pay something, not to protect the TV but to protect yourself from the discomfort of risks. Even though the price of protection is greater than the present value of the expected value of the repairs, it could make you better off. But then you're buying psychological comfort, not financial security. Risk aversion does make it more likely that a person could be made better off by buying protection; but that doesn't mean he or she should be indifferent to the cost of their comfort. Remember, this is economics: Cheap peace of mind is always preferable to expensive peace of mind; and when it gets too expensive, you have actually bought—and I know this sounds crazy—too much peace of mind.

Let's look at our conclusions. Let's review for a moment what we've done today. I took you shopping with me; we went to the mall and we had to decide whether it made sense to buy an extended warranty on a television. That served two purposes for us: First, it was a composite of virtually all of the economic concepts we developed in the past; and it gave us just a small entre, a bridge, into a new topic, behavioral economics, that we're going to explore in the next lecture. But what you should take way from this lecture, however, is this: Even when there's full, data-rich analysis of a decision and it can't be made, it's not possible because it requires too much, thinking like an economist gives us a framework to shape our decisions. It can give us some shortcuts to evaluate the rationality of choices.

In the example of the warranty offer, it was economic thinking that told us we needed to consider: What does our experience tell us about the expected value of future events? It says: What's the role information asymmetry and incentives for blind dates that are created in a situation like that? It reminds us that the timing of costs and the payoffs matter; "when" always matters. It says that the significance of competition, or the lack of competition, is a discipline on players in the game. When we used all that information at our disposal we could evaluate the elements as an essential first step in making a rational choice. We have a framework for thinking rationally, even when we don't have all the hard information necessary to make all the hard calculations. Economic thinking isn't really about providing fixed answers; economic thinking is about knowing what the essential questions are.

In the next lecture, we're going to turn to one last topic, behavioral economics; and we're going to see how some new research on how emotions and perceptions can create obstacles to our own rational decision-making. I think you're going to find that very interesting.

Behavioral Economics—What Are We Thinking?
Lecture 11

When I was young, there was a very famous comic strip named *Pogo Possum*, and one of the most famous quotes out of that was one day when the title character said, "We have met the enemy, and he is us." The strange findings of behavioral economists make that observation applicable here.

B ehavioral economics is a field that crosses the boundary between economic thinking and experimental psychological research. In this relatively new field, we find that the behavior of human beings in both experimental and real-life situations is often very puzzling. The foundation principles and core concepts we've learned envision a world made up of individuals who are always maximizing: They're calculating their options and thinking rationally about how to maximize their self-defined welfare. Yet when actual human behavior is observed, in many different contexts and in many different ways, people seem to make decisions that just don't fit that vision.

A lot of the evidence in behavioral economics comes from carefully controlled experiments run in laboratories where the experimenters will set up structured tasks or games. One of the most famous of these is the ultimatum game, which has shown us an astonishing result: People will often forgo a gain for themselves rather than let someone else become unjustly enriched. Doesn't rationality dictate that you should choose to receive money over not receiving any? Not necessarily; rationality refers to the process of reaching decisions, not to the objectives and motivations. The evidence here is showing us that for many people, fairness has a real value, and unfairness has a real cost. Therefore, rationality requires that their behavior respond to that.

A second puzzling behavior has to do with anchor points. Anchor points are a heuristic that we use, subconsciously, when we find ourselves faced with decisions. Before we go into transactions, we have in our mind conceptions that give us a benchmark of what an appropriate price is. Our psychological anchor points are set by the context in which we live. An anchor point can be an efficient and rational response when we're faced with our inevitable ignorance, but we need to recognize that other people can use them to influence our decisions. Here's an interesting example: Restaurant consultants often suggest that a restaurant add high-priced entrées and wines to its menu to increase the average bill that its diners undertake. Why do they do that? It's not because a lot of people are going

Anchor points impact our spending decisions.

to select the new high-priced options; in fact, the evidence is that the bill rises because those items create a higher anchor point in consumers' minds, making the next-highest-priced option seem more reasonable.

Another surprising finding in behavioral economics is the endowment effect. In the normal economic view, an item's value is determined by its value for me; there's nothing intrinsic about it. But the endowment effect is the opposite of the grass is always greener effect: It says that once the grass is mine, it gets greener. It's hard to think of an economic reason why that should be so, but apparently it is. Another puzzler is something called loss aversion. There's no rational reason why the value we place on $1 won versus $1 lost should be much different, but experimentally we find that a loss hurts about twice as much as a gain helps. This tendency sometimes makes us bypass rational choices that have real expected value gains.

One last behavioral trait is the **status quo effect**. Once we have made a decision, we tend not to revisit it or consider whether it still makes sense. A study done by TIAA-CREF—which is the organization that organizes pensions for college professors—found that half of all college professors never change the allocation of their contributions. Whatever they picked on that first day, they stuck with for their whole career.

What have we learned from the field of behavioral economics? The thing that most prevents us from making rational decisions—the ones prescribed by our economic thinking—is often us. If we really want to make rational decisions, we need to be aware of—and consciously take action to overcome—our intrinsic tendencies toward irrationality. ∎

Important Terms

behavioral economics: A subfield of economics that draws on evidence and techniques taken from social psychology. It focuses on experimental data on how people actually behave when faced with economic decisions.

status quo effect: In behavioral economics, the bias toward not changing once a decision has been made, even if conditions dictate that it would be rational to adapt.

Take-Away Points

1. Social psychology and behavioral economics have uncovered persistent tendencies toward irrationality and bias in human decision making: We adopt subjective anchor points that set parameters for our decisions, we remain attached to past decisions even when they no longer make sense, and we revalue things simply because we possess them.

2. By understanding our biases and tendencies it is possible, and even rational, for us to redefine our (or others') incentive structures to purposefully alter our (or others') decision architecture and overcome our (or others') irrationality.

Behavioral Economics—What Are We Thinking?
Lecture 11—Transcript

Welcome back one more time. Today we're going to go through our 11th lecture in the series on "How to Think Like an Economist." Today we're going to do something just a little bit different: We're going to venture a little deeper into that somewhat new field of behavioral economics, a field that sort of crosses the boundary between economic thinking and experimental psychological research; and I think we're going to find some really strange things there.

In Rogers and Hammerstein's famous classic Broadway story *The King and I*, the Thai monarch has hired a British nanny to come and teach his children; but he finds himself utterly confused by her strange thinking and her strange behavior. At two times during this musical he stops and breaks into a plaintive song that's called "It's a Puzzlement." In this new field of behavioral economics, we're going to find that the actual behavior of real human beings in both experimental situations and some real life situations is also very puzzling; we're going to find some real puzzlement.

The Foundation Principles and the Core Concepts that we've used so far see a world that's made up of individuals who are always maximizing; they're calculating their options, they're thinking carefully about how to maximize their self-defined welfare. People in that world are supposed to be always and everywhere rational in pursuit of that goal. Yet when actual human behavior is observed, in many different contexts and in many different ways, people seem to make decisions that just don't fit that vision. Today, there are some puzzles that we're going to look at, and we're going to see if we can solve these puzzles; if we can explain the behavior using our regular economic way of thinking, or whether they're a challenge to some of these Foundation Principles, Core Concepts, or our Central Conclusions. That's the topic for today.

A lot of the evidence in behavioral economics comes from carefully controlled experiments run in laboratories where the experimenters will set up structured tasks or games; and one of the most famous of these is called the "Ultimatum Game." Here's how it works: Suppose I come to you and

I say, "Would you like $5, no strings attached?" The odds are almost all of us would take it. The options are $5, $0; as the kids say, that's a no-brainer. But let me modify that a little bit: Instead of just giving you the money, what I'd like to do is take all of you and divide you into two groups; one half stays here, the other half goes into another room. I'll pair you so you each have a partner but you don't know who that partner is, and I'm going to link you by computer and you cannot communicate except under very strict circumstances. Now what I'm going to do is I'm going to offer $100 to you as a pair. But there's a catch: You're going to have to agree on how you're going to divide that $100, and you're going to have to do it through a specific process. I'm going to give your partner the power to deliver an ultimatum. He or she will put on your computer screen a take it or leave it split. If you accept that proposal, then each of you gets the money; but if you reject it, neither of you receives anything.

When you first look at it, that seems to be a regular, simple game theory puzzle, and the outcome should be predicted by allowing each of our players to think in economic terms. If you're the one with ultimatum power, your options are to say that, "I can offer very little to my opponent, or I can offer very much; and, of course, anything I offer is greater than zero. He should accept any offer." His payoff matrix says that he should do that; after all, if I offer an ultimatum of $95 for me and $5 for him, that looks easy, doesn't it? Just as it was a moment ago, his options are $5 or $0. That was a no-brainer. Of course $5 is better than nothing; he might be angry, but he'd be unambiguously wealthier. Do you think he'll accept?

When the Ultimatum Game is actually played in an experimental situation, it's astonishing that with a high degree of consistency the person receiving an unfair ultimatum usually will reject it. Apparently the dissatisfaction of letting somebody else benefit from being unfair is so high that people think they're better off forgoing a gain for themselves than for letting someone else become unjustly enriched. That's really interesting; does that challenge the way that economists think? Compared to a payoff of $0, which is what I offered you the first time, either $5 makes you better off or it doesn't make you better off. If you chose $5 in the first instance, doesn't rationality dictate that you should choose it in the second? Not necessarily; remember as far back as Lecture 2 where we first introduced the concept of rationality? In our thinking, rationality refers to the process of reaching decisions, not the objectives and the motivations. If you get great pleasure (or displeasure) from ice fishing, from attending the opera, from sleeping in your hammock, or running an ultra marathon, that's up to you; what you like and appreciate is something that no economist can tell you. What the evidence here is showing us is that there are people—perhaps lots of people—who literally put your money where your mouth is value on social contexts on equity and on fairness. If those things matter to you, like ice fishing matters to you, then rationality as we've been using requires that your behavior respond to that. I guess the evidence from repeated plays of the Ultimatum Game is for many, many people fairness has a real value; unfairness has a real cost. The world's probably a better place because of that. The Ultimatum Game requires that we extend the boundaries of our analysis to pay attention to the social context in which we interact, but it doesn't really undermine the basic tools of our economic thinking.

A second kind of puzzling behavior that comes from behavioral economics is something that has to do with anchor points. Anchor points are a heuristic, a shortcut that people use, apparently subconsciously, when we find ourselves faced with unfamiliar decisions. In the town where I live we have lots of good and successful restaurants; Saturday night is very busy on Main Street. A couple years ago a restaurateur from New York came, and he put a new entry into the dining out sweepstakes. But he didn't last very long; and once he closed down he complained to the local newspaper that apparently people in our town "just don't appreciate fine dining and were not willing to pay for it." What had happened to him was he'd collided with an anchor point. Before we go into transactions, apparently we have in our mind conceptions of anchor points, something that gives us a benchmark to define what an appropriate price to pay. In the early 2000s when the housing bubble was rising so substantially and the San Francisco Bay area was the most expensive housing market in the country, people didn't blink when someone asked $1 million or more for a modest ranch house. But trust me, anyone who moved there from Syracuse, New York where the median home price was about $75,000 would have had a coronary at the mere mention of such a sum. People live in communities where they develop psychological anchor prices set by the context in which they live.

Dan Ariely, one of this new breed of behavior economists, has done a study, and he said that transplants who move from a community like Syracuse to San Francisco take at least a year to adjust their anchor points to the new community. They will undoubtedly have to rent for at least 12 months before they can make the psychological adjustment to realize what an "appropriate" price in the new market is. That failed restaurateur back in Northampton, Massachusetts hadn't recognized that the anchor price for fine dining in a New England college town is going to be a whole lot less than the anchor price in New York City. I think we do appreciate fine dining in our town; we just have a very different definition of what's a reasonable price.

An anchor point can be an efficient and rational response when we're faced with the ignorance that we've talked about before as being inevitable; when information is expensive, we're always going to go into unfamiliar transactions without all the information we'd like, so an anchor point gives us an estimate of what something should cost. But we also need to recognize, if we're realizing how strategic behavior works, that use of anchor points creates strategic opportunities so other people can use them to influence our decisions. Here's an interesting example: Restaurant consultants will often suggest that a restaurant add new very high-priced entrées and high-priced wines to its menu if it wants to increase the average bill that its diners undertake. Why do they do that? It's not because a lot of people are going to select the new high-priced options; in fact, the evidence is that the bill rises because it creates a higher anchor point in consumers' minds because they have something to compare it to, and what happens is it makes the second-highest-priced option seem more reasonable.

Dan Ariely tells another really fascinating tale about anchor points, and in this case he was talking about home bread making machines. When they came on the market a few years ago, that was an absolutely new appliance; no one had experience with them, no one knew how useful they were, no one knew what a reasonable price would be. The manufacturer built the first models and offered them for sale at a price of $275, and they sold like ... well, actually, they didn't really sell much at all. So they went back to the drawing board and what they did was they designed a larger, fancier model, produced it, and priced it at half again as much as the original. They were establishing a high anchor point, a point of comparison; and the result, according to Ariely, is that there were significant increases in sales as a result, not of the deluxe model, but of the base one. That new anchor that was set by the expensive option now made the original machine look like a much better buy; but without experience, without a point of reference, who could possibly tell? I suppose the lesson in all this is that if you want to sell more of an expensive item, maybe you should offer a still more expensive item.

Others try to set anchor points for us in lots of different contexts, and it's probably wise of us to recognize when they are doing that. I like to think that my wife and I are very generous supporters of lots of good causes. I think the fundraisers think we should be even better supporters, because we get any number of letters each year, often with a little personal note at the bottom, saying, "We'd like to have a suggested donation of $1,000." At that point, I usually choke, gag, turn to my wife, and say, "Who do they think we are? We don't have that kind of money?" Then I think a little bit more about what's happening, and I know they don't really expect us to give $1,000; oh they'd like it, but they don't expect it. The purpose of putting the $1,000 suggestion there is to raise our anchor point; and if it makes us decide to give $200 rather than the $100 we were originally considering, the letter served its purpose. It's just like the very high priced wine on the menu: It raised the expectation of what was appropriate.

People can set anchor points strategically for us when we're doing some kind of a guided search. A few years back, my older son and his wife were looking for their first home to buy, and of course they asked dad to come along as a consultant. We noticed that whenever a real estate agent set up a series of houses for us to examine in a day, the first one we went to was always the worst one. It would be in bad shape, it would need lots of repairs, it would be full of clutter, and it would be overpriced. After this had happened two or three times, we realized they never expected us to be seriously interested in that house at all. The purpose of starting there was to set a standard to make all of the others look that much better. The "dump" was on the itinerary to provide an anchor point.

I guess that's done commonly. A few years later when my younger son and his wife started the same kind of a search, I went along with them as well; and I remember the first house we went to was an absolute disaster. The wiring was so bad it couldn't get insured, the roof was about to fall off, and the house was being sold by somebody called "Bob." After that, the semi-serious response that the kids had with every house they looked at was "Well at least it's better than Bob's." That phrase still sticks with them even to this day. Anchors can be very useful tools in understanding situations when we have limited information and limited experience. In that sense, their use can be very rational; but we also know there's a potential for that process to be used strategically by others, and we need to be conscious of that as we make our decisions.

There's another puzzle in behavioral economics, and this one's a bit harder to reconcile with our basic toolkit; it's what's called the endowment effect. In the normal economic view, an item's value, of course—we've said many times—is its value for me; there's nothing intrinsic about it. It measures the contribution to my self-defined welfare on the margin. Remember that desert traveler, stricken with thirst. The question how much water was worth depends on how much he actually had. If I'm in a position where right now a glass of water would be worth $.50 to me at the moment you begin handing it to me, it should still be worth $.50 to me when it reaches my hand; there's no obvious reason why changing possession should alter my valuation. But behavioral economics seems to find that it does. It's the opposite of the grass is always greener effect; the endowment effect is that once the grass is mine, it gets greener. It's hard to think of an economic reason why that should be so, but apparently it is.

Here's a hypothetical: Suppose I had an infallible lie detector, and I hooked you up to that and I offered you a bottle of wine and you said to me, "I'll pay $100 for that and not a penny more." With my economic thinking I would conclude, "Aha! Your marginal value for that bottle of wine is $100," and if immediately after you bought it someone came up to you and said, "I'd like to buy that bottle of wine for $110," normal economic thinking says of course you'd sell; because you have $100 value you just revealed to us, now you're offered $110 for it, it's only logical to sell, seemingly rational. But people don't always behave that way. Apparently a bird in the hand is worth much more than a bird in the bush, or even a bird in someone else's hand; maybe quite a bit more.

Dan Ariely again and one of his colleagues, Ziv Carmon, ran a natural experiment to determine just how strong this endowment effect can be; this is a fascinating outcome. They both teach at Duke University, and Duke periodically finds itself in crucial playoff basketball games that are the highlight of the campus' season. The number of students that can be accommodated in the basketball arena is much fewer than the number of students on campus, so the competition for tickets is intense. Students camp out in line, sometimes for days on end, putting their whole lives on hold not to get game tickets, but to qualify for a lottery number that will let them possibly get game tickets. The actual tickets go to the lottery winners. The lottery winners and the lottery losers all paid the same price, they all camped out for a long period of time, and so it would seem that the difference between the winners and the losers is pure chance. With the logic we were just talking about with the bottle of wine, it would seem like the students who win the lottery tickets, the price for which they would be willing to sell—the absolute minimum price they'd be willing to sell—should be pretty close to the maximum price a loser would be willing to pay. Shouldn't those prices turn out to be the same? Logically you'd think it would, but it turns out that, in fact, they aren't.

Here's what Ariely and Carmon did: They called up all of the losers of the lottery tickets, and they said, "I might be able to find you a ticket, but I need to know what's the absolutely maximum price you could pay, you would not go any higher," and then they were told, "We'll put you on the list and call back if we can find a seller to meet that bid price." It's important that the losers can't understate how much they will pay, because if they do they lose any real chance at those very scare and highly coveted tickets. Then they called the winners and said, "We might have some buyers for your tickets," and so they pushed and pushed and pushed and said, "What's the absolute lowest selling price for which you would sell your tickets? I'll call back if I can find a buyer." Again, the holders of tickets knew that if they overstated their price, what economists call their reservation price, they wouldn't be able to cash in. what do you think the results were? This is very interesting.

The losers said they would pay an average maximum price to buy one of those tickets of $170 each. The winners said the average minimum price they would take to sell one of their tickets wasn't $170, it wasn't even $175, it was $2,400; a huge difference in value that can't be explained because the two groups came from different socioeconomic classes (one was wealthy, one was poor) or different intensity as basketball fans. They'd all camped out for days on end putting their lives on hold; they were all undergraduate students at the same institution. The only thing that separated those two groups of people was chance in a lottery; and the only clear difference is some had won tickets and held them in their hands and some did not, and that alone somehow made the value nearly 11 times higher for the lucky ones. For reasons largely inexplicable by our traditional reasoning, there was a very significant endowment effect. Even if traditional theory can't really explain it, it behooves us to recognize it. As the King of Thailand sang in the show, "It is a puzzlement."

Another puzzle in behavioral economics is something called loss aversion. There's no real reason why the value we place on winning $1 or losing $1 should be much different—it's a dollar in versus a dollar out; the same general thing—but experimentally I guess we find that a loss hurts about twice as much as a gain helps. $100 loss is the negative equivalent in self-defined welfare of a $200 gain; that's found from experimental data. If you don't believe it, visualize the following: Suppose you're on one of these game shows. You've been answering questions correctly and pushing your winnings up and you're up to $50,000. Here comes the final double or nothing question, you risk it all, and you lose. You gained $50,000, a few minutes later you lost $50,000, you are right back where you started; everything canceled out. But are you going to feel worse on the way home than you did on the way to the studio? I'm betting you will; you might not sleep for days. The loss hurt worse than the gain helped. Mathematically nothing changed; you had exactly as much as you went home as you had when you came. But psychologically, everything changed. This tendency, known as "loss aversion," sometimes makes us bypass rational choices that have real expected value gains. We forego chances of substantial benefits because there's a chance of a relatively small loss.

One last behavioral trait today, and that's called the "status quo" effect. My daughter drives a 10-year-old automobile; it wasn't a fancy car to begin with, it has well over 100,000 miles on it. We looked up the Blue Book value not long ago and it was $1,000, maybe $1,100. The comprehensive insurance on that car in case of collision, even with a deductible, is a little bit over $300 a year. With all the things we've talked about and if you look at that rationally, you have two options, and it should be easier to pick: You can take a risk, a chance, of totaling the car and losing as much as $1,100 dollars; or you can absolutely for certain lose $300 each and every year paying that premium. The expected value—we talked about that—for the comprehensive coverage only makes sense if the probability of her totaling that car is greater than about 40 percent. She's a safe driver, and simple expected value analysis says no, that makes no sense.

But, of course, when she first bought that car the calculus was different. It was a newer car, it had lower mileage, the value was greater and the expected value of a loss was greater; at that moment, it probably made sense to cover her. But the car aged, the miles piled up, and the value declined; and clearly there came a point where the falling value of the car made the expected value of the loss so low that the insurance made no sense. But for years she did what we all do: She got a renewal form in the mail, she checked "yes, renew," and gave it not a moment's thought. We tend not to revisit decisions once made or consider whether they still make sense. We experience status quo bias. It was really only a move to a new state last summer that forced her to think seriously about that decision when she had to shop for new insurance among multiple companies.

The consequences of this bias affect lots more than just too much "clunker insurance." When I finished my Ph.D., it was going to be my first salaried job ever; I was going to be an assistant professor of economics. I was 26 years old; I'd been in school my entire life; I'd never had a steady income. Retirement? That was the furthest thing from my mind; I didn't give it a moment's thought. But when I arrived on campus to take that job, I had to fill out lots of forms, and one of them was choose an allocation for your contributions to your retirement plan. I did what most people do: I took the contributions and I split them equally among the alternatives—that seemed like the easy solution—and I forgot completely about it for years. Now, it's many years later, and I'm getting a little bit closer to retirement; and today I realized that there were much better strategies. I should have been more diligent, I should have reallocated my contributions. That first youthful choice I made became the status quo, and I stuck with it for years.

You'd think that a Ph.D. in economics, of all people, would apply the tools of rational analysis and make better decisions than that. That would have been the rational thing to do, but the key phrase in that was "an economist of all people"; and despite my formal training, I made the choice just like everyone else does and got caught by status quo bias. Today I know that it has cost me literally tens of thousands of dollars by not making the best decisions. I'm not alone in that. A study done by TIAA-CREF—which is the organization that organizes pensions for college professors; and remember that college professors are very educated people—found that half of all college professors never, never, ever change the allocation of their contributions, even once. Whatever they picked on that first day, they stuck with for their whole career.

Marketers know this about us. Cable companies and phone companies offer low introductory rates—$19.95 for the first six months—because they know that at the end of six months, we're probably just going to continue even at the higher rate. Magazine publishers know this; they try to get us to subscribe just once, so they know that we're likely to keep renewing automatically, even if we never even read the magazine. Manufacturers prefer rebates to price reductions; do you know why? Because most of us don't even send in the forms to claim the rebates that enticed us to go in and make the purchase in the first place.

What are the conclusions? When I was young, there was a very famous comic strip named "Pogo Possum," and one of the most famous quotes out of that was one day when the title character said, "We have met the enemy, and he is us." The strange findings of behavioral economists make that observation applicable here. The evidence is pretty clear: The thing that most prevents us from making rational decisions—the ones described by our economic thinking—is often us. That's the real take away point from this lecture: If we really want to make rational decisions, we need to be aware of, and consciously take action to overcome, our own intrinsic tendencies toward irrationality. We're susceptible to being influenced by anchor points that others can set strategically; we treat equal losses and gains as if somehow they're very different; our inertia lets unwise decisions persist; we leave free money on the table.

On one level, the ubiquity of these very strange behaviors muddies up the waters; it makes economists' predictions of rational behavior seem just a bit out of focus. But on another level, when we become conscious of these phenomena, it gives us an opportunity to do some things to overcome our own irrationality. We now know what an anchor point is, and if we recognize when someone is doing something to set one for you, you can resist being unduly influenced. When you go into a restaurant, be careful not to compare the entrée price and the wine price with the highest items, compare them to the lowest. When the real estate agent says, "Let's start out with this dump as a starting point," skip that house, because it's just trying to set an anchor point. You can even make status quo bias work for you. Here's a suggestion: When you sign up for that new cable service with six months' low rate, that same day write a letter canceling the new cable service, give it to a friend, give that friend $5, and say, "Mail this in six months unless I explicitly ask you not to." You can even do something like this: Suppose you make an agreement with a close friend that each year you'll get together to celebrate your birthday, and you promise you'll pay for any bottle of wine on the menu that your friend chooses if you have not in the past month met with your financial advisor to consider your retirement allocations. Two economists, Rich Thaler and Cass Sunstein, call these things "nudges"; conscious changes that we make to our own "choice architecture" that we can create new incentives for ourselves to make us make more rational decisions.

We're almost to the end, my friends. The next time, we're going to take a multipart final exam. We'll take a look at a few other nudges that have come along as a final way to see how we can think like economists. We'll take out our tools and our concepts, we'll take one last look at them, we'll examine them, and then we'll use them to look at a couple of large policy issues and a couple of small personal decisions to see how effectively we've learned to think like economists.

Acting like an Economist
Lecture 12

To think like an economist is to accede to a particular paradigm shift that forever changes the world in which you live.

It's time for our final exam. Let's see if you can think like an economist about some complex real-world issues. First, how can you think like an economist about crime? In 1992, Gary Becker won a Nobel Prize in Economics in part for applying economic thinking to the question of crime and punishment. Leaving aside things like serial murder and crimes of passion, Becker argued that criminals are just like the rest of us: Crime can be a rational individual choice. First, you look at opportunity cost. What's the highest legal earning you could have? Compare that, then, to the criminal option. That analysis must include the expected value of legal punishment, which depends on both the probability of conviction and the sentence that might be incurred. Not surprisingly, there's evidence that the amount of criminal activity does in fact depend on both the certainty and the severity of punishment.

Thinking like an economist helps you weigh options that carry uncertain outcomes.

Another complex question is what is the rational response to our irrationality? Behavioral economics shows us that we systematically make irrational decisions about our futures. Is there a way we could use our understanding of incentives to promote better outcomes for ourselves? One example is retirement plans in which your employer will match funds that you contribute. The match being offered is free money, but an astonishing number of people, perhaps due to status quo bias, fail to take advantage of it. What if we redesigned the incentive structure some way, such as changing the default position so that all employees are automatically enrolled in their retirement plan? Economists are starting to recognize that society can find ways to nudge people to make better choices.

Economists are starting to recognize that society can find ways to nudge people to make better choices.

What about nudging yourself? Let's look at a puzzle that lots of economists have examined: Many people buy annual health club memberships and then go so infrequently that it would be cheaper to pay by the day. Could you change your own incentive structure to alter your future behavior? Here's a strategy: Join a health club with a friend, and sign a contract with him agreeing to pay each other a $25 fine each week that you fail to work out 3 times. If both of you go 3 or more times, no money changes hands. If neither of you shows up, the money goes into a fund that goes to the person who next receives a payment. Our knowledge of loss aversion says that the direct $25 marginal cost of skipping the gym is a strong motivator. You changed your incentives to counter your irrationality, and you could wind up healthier—and possibly wealthier.

Now that we've reached the end of this course, I hope you have a clear understanding of what it means to think like an economist. I know that you have the tools you need to do just that. Thinking like an economist does not mean that you have well-defined, memorized rules and answers to any question that can arise; it means you have a framework that can provide you with the questions necessary to think your way through—to analyze and reason your way to an important decision. It's all about seeing the world in a particular way and improving the decisions you make in that world. This lecture wasn't actually your final exam; the final test of your ability to think like an economist is going to be what you do with these tools as you confront the many personal, business, and policy decisions in your life. I do sincerely hope that you do well on that exam, because it's the only one that really matters. ∎

1. Thinking like an economist does not mean having memorized answers or strict decision rules. It means viewing the world from a particular perspective and seeing problems and issues within a specific framework. It defines questions; it does not dictate final answers.

2. The usefulness of economic thinking extends far beyond narrow economic issues such as the future world price of oil. It is a framework that can bring sense to problems as complex as choking traffic congestion, as pressing as high rates of crime, as pervasive as global climate change, and as personal as linking your children's allowance to completion of their chores.

Acting like an Economist
Lecture 12—Transcript

And so here we are, one last time. Today we're going to have the final lecture in our course on "How to Think Like an Economist." By now I expect you know that economists think like economists about virtually everything they see. Obviously it helps them make sense of changes in interest rates; it helps them understand what happens to the price of oil; it certainly helps them understand income tax revenues. But you should also see that by now economists think their thinking helps them make sense of crime, commitments to their own future physical fitness, and questions like traffic congestion. To think like an economist is to accede to a particular paradigm shift that forever changes the world in which you live. You'll always see the world as a different place once you've adopted this particular lens. In this lecture, what I want to do is first take out these tools one time, we can sharpen them up just a little bit; and then, just to make sure that we're comfortable with them, we'll see how they work in a few distinct contexts. Then after today, you're going to have to apply them on your own, because once you "graduate" from this course, I'm not going with you. But I think you're well-equipped by now to do the economic thinking all on your own.

What's the first step in our last journey here? The first step is to do an inventory; let's take all our tools out, make sure they're at the ready. Then I'm going to pose to you a few questions, a final exam of sorts, to see whether you're comfortable or not in using these tools. So you recall, back at the beginning we started with six Foundation Principles. They're really very simple, and they're really pretty much self-evident to anybody who looks for them; but together they're really quite profound. Many, many mistakes and many bad decisions result from failing to remember these six things: First, people respond to incentives. You change incentives, behavior will respond. Second, there is no such thing as a free lunch; in a world of scarcity, life is about opportunity costs and making tradeoffs. The third principle: There are at least two sides to every interaction, and wisdom requires that you be able to see the incentives on all sides from all participants. The next principle is that everything affects everything else. There are always going to be unanticipated impacts coming at us from all directions. The fifth principle: For any action, there's the danger of significant unintended consequences.

Then finally, in this world of complex interrelationships, no one is really in control.

Then, with those principles in mind, we developed three Core Concepts to give those principles context. The first one was that economists think in terms of rationality. Economic thinking doesn't really tell you what a good objective is; it just tells you how to make choices to achieve the objectives you have. Rational decisions are decisions made strategically; constantly choosing better alternatives, in terms of self-defined welfare, over worse alternatives. The second concept was that economists tend to focus their attention on marginal analysis. Our lives are made up of sequences of small changes; they're decisions made on the margin in small pieces. Insights come—if you think back to my silly example—from focusing on the teaspoons going back and forth rather than the salt and pepper shakers. You never decide what you're going to do with the rest of your life; you may think you are, but in fact mostly what you're doing is choosing what to do with the next small piece of it. Life is the uncontrolled sum of all those smaller choices. The third concept we talked about was optimization: the process of making small adjustments on the margin, trading a little bit for a little bit of that, until we've squeezed as much as we possibly can; we've optimized, we've maximized subject to constraints.

Finally, we reached the central conclusion that individual rational decisions can, if conditions are just right, lead to results that are socially efficient. Any time there's a better alternative—a change, a move, an interaction—that's an unambiguous gain for a decider, our rationality principle says they should choose it. It also says rational individuals will interact—they'll trade, they'll contract, they'll cooperate—only if it makes all of them better off. When there are no unambiguous moves left to take, when there are no mutually beneficial adjustments on the margin, when there is no money left on the table, the outcome is efficient. It's not unambiguously perfect; it's not necessarily in any meaningful philosophical sense just; but it is efficient. That's the lens through which economists view the world. In the first lecture, I postulated that if I'd had an artist and a geologist looking with me at a mountain in the Pacific Northwest, we would all literally "see" different things. When an economist looks at the mountain or anything else, all of what we've just talked about is what he or she is seeing.

We also had to realize that much of the world falls short of the conditions; conditions aren't always just right to lead to efficiency. We might not have enough information, because information itself is costly; it would be irrational and inefficient for us to try to acquire it all. We face problems with unavoidable, probabilistic risks. We know that there can be distortions created for us when others use information strategically. In the last lecture, we spoke at some length how behavioral economists tell us that even when we could act rationally and could act efficiently, inexplicably often we do not. The tools are imperfect, there is distortion in the lens; but those of us who are committed to the discipline, to the paradigm, are persuaded that the vision provided by thinking like an economist helps to make clear what would otherwise be in many cases a confusing fog.

The tools are out, they're ready; it's time for the final exam: Three multipart questions to see if you can think like an economist about some real world issues. Question number one's going to be an essay question about the economics of crime. How can you think like an economist about crime? Let me propose a question to you: If you were late for a very important appointment, you only saw one parking space and it was in a tow zone, would you park there? What if the chance of being towed was 50 percent? 10 percent? 2 percent? What if you knew that the tow truck drivers were on strike? If the decision you make is dependent upon those probabilities of being towed, I welcome you to the world of rational crime; because after all, the violation of the law was the same in each case, the benefit to you was the same in each case, the only difference was the expected cost of the punishment. If your decision to abide by the law depends on the costs and benefits rather than some inviolable moral imperative then you have demonstrated two things: First, even potential criminals can think like economists from time to time; and perhaps maybe rational economists can turn into criminals.

In 1992, Gary Becker won a Nobel Prize in Economics, in part for applying our economic tools—our tools of economic thinking— to these questions of crime and its punishment. He had to leave aside the inexplicable evils like serial murder and crimes of passion, but other than that, Becker argued, criminals are just like the rest of us; crime for many people, he said, is just a rational, individual choice. So in your essay, what kinds of things should you cover? First, you'll want to talk about opportunity cost. What's the highest legal earning? If you're engaging in criminal activity, what are you not doing that's legal? You'd have to compare that, then, to the criminal option; and, of course, the criminal option would depend on chance events like what's the expected value of the legal option? What's the expected value of the punishment? Of course, that expected value depends both on the sentence that might be incurred and the probability of conviction.

Not surprisingly, economists have studied these issues; and there's evidence that, in fact, the amount of criminal activity does depend both on the certainty and the severity of punishment. Steven Levitt, who's one of the coauthors of the best-selling book *Freakonomics*, did a study of what happens to criminal behavior of teenagers as they start to approach that age boundary where they're no longer covered by the relatively lenient juvenile courts and they start to fall under the auspices of the much harsher adult criminal justice system. He's an economist; he was not at all surprised to find that as the certainty and severity of the punishment rose, the commission of crimes fell apace. Changes in incentives cause changes in behavior; for rational criminals, when crime truly doesn't pay, there will be much less of it.

Let's have a pop quiz: Another part of the criminal justice question is recidivism; criminals seem to come back again after they've been punished for the first crime. Let's assume that Becker's analysis is true; let's talk about what happens in the future. You've been caught; you've been convicted; that probably means you weren't that good at crime. If you think like an economist about what effects that prison sentence is going to have upon you after release, maybe that will help explain some of the high rates of recidivism. Obviously there are many factors involved in this, but one is that while you're a convicted felon, you have lots of time to devote to learning from your fellow inmates better, more productive criminal techniques. You have a higher education on how to be a more productive criminal. Second, once you've been released, the fact that you have a felony conviction on your record reduces probably the legal earnings that you'll be able to acquire. Conviction for the first crime changes the incentive, changes the relative payoff from committing the second; changes the calculus and the rationality of crime.

Having thought about that, now what? To balance that change in calculus, the criminal justice system commonly decides to increase penalties for repeat offenders; they're trying to come back with higher incentives in a negative sense. Some states have even gone so far as to adopt rigid three strikes laws: a mandatory life sentence without parole for any third felony conviction. That raises lots of issues that involve justice and ethics, and I'm going to leave those for someone another day; and it does raise the cost of later crimes up to a point. But an economist looking at that incentive structure would see something very specific, because when an economist faces an issue, where does he or she always go? They look at the margin; and when you look at the margin, what do you see? What incentives does that three strikes law create for a two time loser? If the state does not have a death penalty, the cost of that third crime is everything. The fourth one is free. Get caught committing an armed robbery, the penalty is life without parole. Kill the victim to reduce the chance of getting caught and identified and the maximum penalty is still life without parole. Then kill a police officer to avoid capture and the maximum penalty remains life without parole. The marginal cost of the murders is zero; that's an inescapable economic incentive that economists say it behooves us to consider.

Question number two on the final exam: What's the rational response to our own irrationality? Remember when we looked at behavioral economics, we found lots of evidence that people seem systematically to make irrational decisions about their very own futures. Is there some way we could use our understanding of incentives to promote even better outcomes for ourselves or for others in the future? I think it's clear that virtually anyone who has access to an employer-sponsored retirement plan where the employer will match funds that you put in would be well-advised to take advantage of that. The match being offered is free money; it's lying there on the table. Old You is going to be very glad if Young You makes the wise, rational choice and picks that money up. Nevertheless, an astonishing number of people, perhaps suffering from status quo bias, fail ever to do so. All they have to do is go in the office, file a paper, and they pick up that great financial advantage, a costless gain. But apparently knowing it's a good idea is not enough for us to take advantage of it.

What if we redesigned the incentive structure some way; maybe we find a way to push them—or perhaps ourselves—into choices that I think we'd all agree are better, but somehow we just don't get around to making? Richard Thaler and Cass Sunstein again talk about the design of "choice architectures" in their very interesting book *Nudge*. They say that they're adopting a policy of "libertarian paternalism"; they want everybody to be free to make his or her own decision about healthcare, about retirement savings, about using of credit, and about organ donation. But they say that all decision structures have a default position, what would happen if you don't get around to making an explicit choice; and they think maybe we should find ways to change the default positions, to nudge people to make better choices. All retirement plans have a choice architecture; but what Thaler and Sunstein argue is that knowing this, maybe we should consciously change the direction in which people are affected. If they didn't behave in such irrational and puzzling ways, we wouldn't have to do that; but now we do. With most retirement plans, you have to go in and sign up; you have to take steps to participate. You have to opt in; you have to file the paperwork. But instead what if we set up retirement plans where employees are automatically enrolled unless they make a conscious decision to opt out, where they have to come in and sign the papers to withdraw; participation when those kinds of systems are established is much higher. Nobody's forced to stay in the program, nobody has to make a choice they didn't want make. But sometimes being rational seems to require just a little bit of help. Economists are coming to recognize that.

What about nudging yourself? What if there's no benevolent Human Resources executive who can change the incentives for you? Could your wise self create incentives to make your foolish self come out with better choices? There's a puzzle that lots of economists have examined: An awful lot of people buy annual health club memberships, and then go so infrequently that it would have been cheaper to pay by the day. Obviously, at the beginning we intend, we expect, we hope that we're going to show up and exercise a lot more than we do. But day by day we make short term decisions that aren't consistent with our long term desires. How's this for Part B of Question Two? Could you purposefully change your own incentive structure to alter your own future behavior; can you nudge yourself? How's this for an option: Join a health club with a friend, and you and he can sign a contract; and you agree that at the end of any week when you have not gone three times, you will pay him a direct $25 fine, here you are, cash on the barrel head. If both of you go three or more times, no money changes hands; there's no cost to either. If neither of you shows up, the money goes into a fund and it all goes to the first person who shows up three times a week when the other one does not.

Our knowledge of loss aversion, our knowledge of behavioral economics, says that the direct $25 marginal cost of taking a day off is a very strong motivator. If you behave as you both intended when you purchased the contract, it doesn't cost you anything. If you're diligent and your contract partner is not, the monetary gain plus the better healthful result, he might even end up paying for your membership for you. In that case, you are both healthier and wealthier, and you changed your own incentives to counter your own irrationality. You induced yourself to change your behavior. You planted your own carrots; you wielded your own stick. Interesting. Perhaps some health club could market that kind of a plan to attract new members.

Do you think anyone would ever really do a thing like that? I have a friend—an economist friend, of course—who did something like that to help him cut back on his smoking. His resolve was always strong, but his craving became stronger. He thought he should do something to make the marginal cost of a cigarette higher so his recalcitrant self would start meeting the standards his resolved self wanted him to live up to. Our offices were pretty far from any commercial source of cigarettes; he couldn't just run down and pick up pack of smokes. So he'd buy one pack of cigarettes, give them to the department secretary, and instruct her: "Sell me cigarettes for $5 yet, not a penny less, no exceptions no matter what I beg." The money would go to the National Cancer Society. He did reduce his smoking because he chose to find a way to make each marginal cigarette that much more expensive directly for himself.

The final's almost over; let's take a stab at just one last issue, and that means we're going to spend some time stuck in traffic. If you started to think like an economist, and you mull over some of these issues while you're driving, you probably have plenty of time to do that. Cities all over the world are choking in traffic; countless hours are lost to delay and congestion; more and more and more cars try to drive on roads that have no greater capacity. Estimates are that in the United States the average commuter spends 40 hours a year in delay on the highway; that's an entire work week of time sitting in the highway in congested traffic. That's nuts; why do we put up with it? How can we fix it? Those are good questions, but let's take a minute and think like economists about them.

Traffic congestion is a social outcome; and economists think social outcomes are the result of individuals making decisions based on the incentives that face them at the time of their choice. Of course, the incentive for most drivers, for most travelers, is to get from here to there at the lowest possible total cost; not defined by dollars paid out—we're economists now, remember—we want to use the true currency: a cost as a reduction in my self-defined welfare. Time, hassle, discomfort, noise, inconvenience, and the risk of crime are all real costs. People make the choice of how to travel that minimizes those costs; it's only rational. Not economists and not transportation planners can tell them how they should value them.

In the 1960s, San Francisco began constructing the Bay Area Rapid Transit System, the BART system. It was the first time we tried to reimpose and build onto an automobile age city an underground rail system. The designers who built that started with one crucial design assumption, and they explicitly stated this in the plan: "Commuters' greatest concern," they said, "will be the speed of travel once on board." They could not have been more wrong. Since that time, there have been multiple studies, and they all conclude just exactly the opposite. An extra 20 minutes once on the train hurts far less than an extra 20 minutes looking for a parking place, transferring from the bus, standing on the platform waiting. To commuters, they have now shown in study after study, hassle time costs a lot more than pure time. BART's design, with widely spaced stations located out on the edges of population concentrations, meant hassle is a large part of each and every trip.

But a car, now that's the whole package. It leaves from my driveway when I'm ready to go; it goes directly to my destination and I don't have to transfer; I pick the music; I control the temperature. That's the way to drive. This probably explains why such a large share of the riders when BART opened weren't leaving their cars to get on BART, they were switching from buses. It was better as an alternative to the bus than it was to the car. BART turned out to be the rational choice for far fewer commuters than the planners had hoped.

What about the social consequences? If driving is the best individually rational decision, why is the social result so utterly insane? Or in economic terms, so inefficient? Why does the Bay Bridge turn into a linear parking lot for hours on end? That, of course, is the second part of the final exam question here; and to answer it, we're going to dig down into our toolkit and we're going to pull out two of the things we discussed in earlier lectures: marginal analysis and the tragedy of the commons. How much delay does a marginal car cause when it enters into the highway? The answer, of course, is that always depends; it depends on how many other cars are already on the highway. If you're pulling onto a near-empty road, no one has to slow down; if you're pulling onto a road with lots of cars, then not only does the new car have to slow down and be delayed while trying to merge with traffic, so are all the other cars behind on the road; they must all adapt. Traffic engineers tell us that at some point, one minute of delay for the marginal car—the car entering the highway—causes enough backup that the total delay for all the other cars is greater than one hour; one minute of delay for the marginal car, one hour of delay for everybody else on the road.

Now we have the insanity. The marginal price paid by the new car isn't equal to the true marginal cost. Driving, often alone, does make sense for each of us individually but not for us collectively. The price we pay is a lie. Pogo Possum was right when he said, "We have met the enemy and he is us." It's our own rationality and the decisions based on it that lead to our collective inefficiency because the price, because the incentive, does not reflect the true cost.

How about an extra credit pop quiz? Before I talk for a minute about the solutions to all this, let's talk about a case in the real world. Mexico City has world-class congestion and some of the worst urban air in the world. According to the World Health standards, pollution in Mexico City exceeds the minimum standards over 90 percent of the time; something needs to be done. In 1989, the Mexican government thought it had a plan: It put in a rolling ban on driving based on license plate numbers; so on Mondays, any car whose license plate ended in a five or a six could not legally be driven between 5 am and 10 pm. Other days of the week, other numerals dominated. In theory, that should have reduced the number of cars on the roads of Mexico City by almost half a million each day; in theory. But now you're a pretty sophisticated economist: That change in policy changed incentives; it probably had unintended consequences. Do you have any ideas what you might predict?

Clearly not being able to drive your car is a major inconvenience. You can grumble, stay at home, adapt; you might be able to find some way around it; you might ride the bus; or you might buy a second car, a car with a license plate with a different numeral. You'd have your Tuesday car, or you'd have your Friday car; and apparently a lot of the citizens of Mexico City did that. There was no measurable improvement in the measured air quality; there was an increase in the registered cars in the metropolitan area; and of course, most of those cars were older, less efficient used cars, and they worked against the proponents who were trying to use that as a clean air system. When the government imposed the ban they were thinking like lawyers, they were trying to dictate a change in behavior, rather than like economists trying to figure out how to induce one.

That's the last part of the last question: How would an economist solve the overuse of roads? That's right down to the basics: If you want to change people's behavior, change their incentives; change the price. There have been some experiments in various cities in the world using congestion pricing. In 2003, London established a system of congestion pricing in the core of the city; it charged a daily price to enter this designated congestion zone. It wasn't a trivial price: It's about $15 per entry; and you have to pay it before you enter the zone, so you have to plan ahead. You can pay it by computer; you can pay it by cell phone. Cameras record the license plates of everybody entering that zone, and if you drive in it without first, ahead of time, paying the fee, you'll be fined about $200. Trust me, that is a change in cost; that is a change in incentives. Not surprisingly for economists, that meant a change in driving decisions and traffic delays and congestion in the core of London have been significantly impacted by that.

Most economists say that's a good start but that's a blunt tool, because actually the congestion changes dramatically from one day to the next; what it is on Tuesday won't be exactly what it's going to be on Wednesday. Their optimal economic policy would be to vary the congestion price. They'd like to have an effective guide to efficient decisions, so the price should change hour to hour, day to day, condition to condition so that it reflects the specific cost of a particular trip. Sounds like science fiction, but not really; all you really need is some kind of a variant of a GPS monitor, and then you can see on the screen what the variable congestion charge in real time is. It would be like a taxi meter, and you'd say, "If I take this trip it will cost me $2.40." That would be an inconvenience, it would be an aggravation when we find that we have to alter some of our plans for our low value trips; but oh, my friends, it would be a blessing when we could take our high volume trips on less-congested roads.

And so we've come to the end of this course, and I hope that by now you have a clear understanding of what it means to think like an economist. I know that you have the tools you need to do just that whenever it seems really appropriate. Thinking like an economist does not mean that you have well-defined, memorized rules and answers to any question that can arise; what thinking like an economist means is that you have a framework that can provide you with the questions necessary to think your way through, analyze, and reason your way to an important decision. It's all about seeing the world in a particular way, and perhaps sometimes improving the rationality of the decisions you make in that world. Despite what I said at the beginning about this lecture being the final exam, that's not really true; the final test of your ability to think like an economist is going to be what you do with these tools as you confront the many personal, business, and policy decisions in your life. I do sincerely hope that you do well on that exam, because that's the only one that really matters.

Glossary

adverse selection: When the incentives in a situation result in the elimination of the best alternatives, leaving only less desirable options (e.g., when uncertainty about quality drives the best used cars from the market, leaving the lemons).

behavioral economics: A subfield of economics that draws on evidence and techniques taken from social psychology. It focuses on experimental data on how people actually behave when faced with economic decisions.

butterfly effect: In chaos theory, the hypothesis that small events can be linked through distant causal chains to seemingly unrelated events (e.g., the beating of a butterfly's wings would theoretically set in motion a chain of events that would lead to a change in a distant weather pattern).

compound interest: Interest earned based on the sum of the original principal plus interest accrued. Interest earned in one period is added to the principal for the next period. Over time, interest is increasingly being earned on interest from earlier periods. The result is exponential growth in total dollar value.

constrained maximization: *See* **optimization**.

discount rate: The percent by which an event's present value is diminished as the event moves further into the future. The higher the discount rate, the greater the value placed on current, as opposed to future, events.

discounted present value: The current equivalent value of an event that will not occur until sometime in the future. The further away an event is, and the higher the discount rate, the lower its current, or discounted, present value.

expected value: Formally, it is the sum of the payoffs from all possible outcomes, each multiplied by the probability of its occurrence. In essence, it is the average outcome that would result from repeating the same decision multiple times.

future value: The dollar value at some point in the future of funds held today. Because of compounding interest, each dollar today will compound to more than a dollar in the future. The further into the future, the greater the future value.

information asymmetry: A situation in which one party to a transaction has access to information not available, but important, to another party.

information cascade: A growing group assessment of a situation where all members are uninformed of actual facts but form opinions based on the number of others who assert something to be true. Once this process has begun, people still undecided about the truth of the proposition in question view each new adherent as evidence of the proposition's truth.

law of unanticipated influences: A principle that asserts that in a complex interdependent system, it is impossible to anticipate all the external influences and impacts that will alter conditions.

marginal value: The change in a starting total value from a slight increase or decrease in an activity. If a bus company provides service between 2 cities, the marginal cost is the addition to cost of taking on 1 more passenger. The marginal revenue is the increase in revenue from selling the final ticket.

nominal value: The value of anything expressed in dollars unadjusted for inflation. If the nominal price of something is $100, it is impossible to determine if that is high or low without knowing the purchasing power of a dollar.

opportunity cost: The value of the next-best thing that must be given up when time or resources are devoted to one use. It is what is forgone.

optimization (a.k.a. **constrained maximization**): The process of deriving as much benefit as possible within a given limit, for example, deriving the maximum possible benefit from a fixed income.

paradigm: In the framework for understanding science first proposed by Thomas Kuhn, a paradigm is a shared worldview held by practitioners of a given science.

present value: *See* **discounted present value**.

price index: The proportionate cost of a given typical consumer market basket of goods relative to some arbitrary base year denoted as 100. A price index of 127 means that compared to the base year, it now takes 27% more dollars to buy the same bundle of goods.

probability: The probability of any event (e.g., getting heads in a coin toss) is 1 divided by the number of total possible outcomes. In the case of a coin toss, the probability of heads is 1/2.

randomness: A situation where the outcome cannot be predicted with accuracy. Each succeeding event is not correlated with the one before it, so the outcome depends only on chance.

rationality: In economics, rationality means always choosing from among available options the one that provides the greatest net gain. It refers to the process of making choices, not to the objective sought.

real value: The value of anything expressed in constant dollars, adjusted for inflation. A price index is used to deflate or convert nominal to real dollars.

real value of money: Money that has been adjusted to remove the effects of inflation or deflation. Using real money allows comparisons of actual value over time.

risk: The degree to which an outcome depends on probability because future events cannot be perfectly predicted.

risk aversion: A preference for a certain option over a risky option with an identical expected value. Risk aversion stems from psychological discomfort arising from the mere existence of risk.

status quo effect: In behavioral economics, the bias toward not changing once a decision has been made, even if conditions dictate that it would be rational to adapt.

subjective probability: What one perceives to be the likelihood of a probabilistic event. Without complete information, or because of psychological distortions, people can believe events to be more or less likely than they objectively are.

time value of money: The monetary value of an event or product adjusted for when it occurs or exists. *See also* **discounted present value**, **future value**.

uncertainty: Any situation in which there is less than perfect information. Increases and improvements in information reduce uncertainty.

Bibliography

Ariely, Dan. *Predictably Irrational.* New York: Harper Collins, 2008. This is a wonderfully written summary of many of the findings of behavioral economics, the topic of Lecture 11. It documents many of our peculiar irrationalities and the ways in which others can strategically use these to alter our decisions and behaviors.

Bernstein, Peter L. *Against the Gods: The Remarkable Story of Risk.* New York: Wiley, 1996. This book tells the story of the creation of insurance as a means to spread risk. It is the concepts of probability and expected value, and the collection of data on possible losses, that make insurance possible. It is a fascinating story and excellent background for Lecture 7.

Harford, Tim. *The Logic of Life: The Rational Economics of an Irrational World.* New York: Random House, 2008. Harford, a columnist for the *Financial Times* and frequent contributor to National Public Radio, tries to uncover the hidden rationality in situations that at first appear irrational. From Las Vegas poker tournaments to teenage sexual behavior to divorce to executive compensation, Harford finds rationality as a key explanatory force.

———. *The Undercover Economist.* New York: Random House, 2007. In this book, Harford uses economic thinking to explain everyday phenomena, ranging from the cost of your morning coffee to the pervasiveness of poverty in undeveloped economies.

Iowa Electronic Markets website. http://www.biz.uiowa.edu/iem. This website, discussed in Lecture 6, is a mechanism for gathering, collating, and compressing widely scattered information.

Kindleberger, Charles, Robert Aliber, and Robert Solow. *Manias, Panics, and Crashes: A History of Financial Crises.* 5th ed. New York: Wiley, 2005. This is the classic historical analysis of how financial bubbles develop, mature, and ultimately collapse. Rather than learn from past experience, we seem to repeat past mistakes, often with tragic consequences.

Levitt, Steven, and Stephen Dubner. *Freakonomics: A Rogue Economist Explores the Hidden Side of Everything.* New York: Harper Collins, 2005. In this bestseller, Levitt and Dubner find economic forces behind a wide variety of phenomena. They use statistical analyses of sumo wrestling tournaments to conclude that the wrestlers must at times collude. They use the same logical argument to prove that some school teachers responded to incentives to improve student scores by changing student answers. Economic thinking, they argue, can be used to explain the incomes of drug dealers and the elements of effective parenting. Often controversial, this book is always provocative.

Poundstone, William. *Prisoner's Dilemma.* New York: Doubleday, 1997. This book traces the development of game theory in the 1940s and 1950s and then applies it to a number of situations. Used to form national strategy during the Cold War, game theory is applicable to topics as diverse as bidding strategies in auctions and understanding thematic plots in literature.

Schelling, Thomas. *Micromotives and Macrobehavior.* New York: W. W. Norton, 1978. This is one of the earliest books in which an economist tries to use the powers of economic thinking to explore the connection between individual rational choices and less than optimal social outcomes in everyday life. Ranging from the choice of seats in an auditorium to issues of neighborhood racial segregation, Schelling shows how interdependent rational choices do not always lead to desirable results.

Shiller, Robert J. *Irrational Exuberance.* 2nd ed. New York: Doubleday, 2005. This is a classic in the field of financial volatility. Its examination of past and current crises includes some of the psychological forces that drive markets. It covers bubbles and panics in both financial and real estate markets.

Sunstein, Cass. *Risk and Reason: Safety, Law, and the Environment.* Cambridge: Cambridge University Press, 2002. This book focuses primarily on public policy making around issues that involve serious risks of either direct or environmental harm. Sunstein argues for thinking carefully (like an economist) about the marginal benefits and costs of safety regulation. He also develops the idea of cascades as socially created distortions of information about risk.

Surowiecki, James. *The Wisdom of Crowds.* New York: Doubleday, 2004. This book explores ways and contexts in which the judgments or estimates of many people can be combined to produce judgments that are more accurate than those of individual experts. Whether estimating the weight of an ox or the location of a lost submarine, averaged independent estimates prove accurate.

Taleb, Nassim Nicholas. *The Black Swan: The Impact of the Highly Improbable.* New York: Random House, 2007. The title refers the astonishment of British ornithologists upon seeing their first black swan from Australia. All English swans are white, and early naturalists assumed that all swans everywhere were white. Taleb uses this as a metaphor for failure to account for the possibility of catastrophic outcomes simply because we have not yet experienced them. The validity of expected value (discussed in Lecture 7) as a measure depends on accurately including all possible outcomes.

Thaler, Richard H., and Cass Sunstein. *Nudge: Improving Decisions about Health, Wealth, and Happiness.* New Haven: Yale University Press, 2008. This book provides a blueprint for "libertarian paternalism," their term for purposefully designing choice architectures to nudge people to voluntarily make wiser decisions. One of many examples is making participation in a retirement plan the default that people must explicitly opt out of. Those plans have much higher participation rates than otherwise identical programs for which people must take explicit steps to opt in.

Notes